JUDSON PRESS
PUBLISHERS SINCE 1824

S'more Time With GOD

Nancy Ferguson

JUDSON PRESS

PUBLISHERS SINCE 1824

VALLEY FORGE, PA

Unless otherwise indicated, Scripture quotations are the author's paraphrase.

Scripture quotations marked CEV are taken from the Contemporary English Version © 1991, 1992, 1995 by American Bible Society. Used by permission.

Interior design by Beth Oberholtzer
Cover design by Wendy Ronga at Hampton Design Group,
    www.hamptondesigngroup.com

Library of Congress Cataloging-in-Publication Data

Ferguson, Nancy, 1934–
    S'more time with God / Nancy Ferguson. — 1st ed.
        p. cm.
    ISBN 978-0-8170-1663-0 (pbk. : alk. paper) 1. Camping—Prayers and
devotions. 2. Families—Prayers and devotions. 3. Bible—Devotional litera-
ture. 4. Nature—Biblical teaching—Prayers and devotions. I. Title. II. Title:
Some more time with God.
    BV4596.C3F47   2011
    249—dc22

                                                              2010049182

Printed in the U.S.A.

First Edition, 2011.

To E, Sara, and Andrew

*Thanks for all the memories of
days and nights in our tent of meeting.*

Contents

Preface

My kids—now grown—still laugh about it. The first meal of any family camping trip was always Spam, boxed macaroni and cheese, and canned green beans. It was quick and easy and could be on the table within thirty minutes of pulling into a campsite. Who knows how it got to be a tradition? The advent of the meal is now lost in the misty past, but its memory lingers on.

It is a reminder of the many times we packed the car, hitched up the camper, and took off on an adventure. The rhythm of each trip was the same—including that first meal—holding the experiences together in one piece. Backing the camper into the exact right spot, cranking up the roof, pulling out the beds, attaching the tent cover, and putting everything in its place were processes repeated again and again. We enjoyed long walks in nature, conversation around the campfire, hot cocoa on cold nights, and books read together curled up in the red sleeping bag. At the end of each camping time, we repeated the rhythm of taking down the camper and leaving for home.

Yet each trip was unique, depending on the setting, the length of the trip, and the things we did together. Over the years we found a temporary home in the desert, among the pines, and by the shores of the roaring sea. Sometimes we left right after church and came home by dinner on Monday; sometimes we were gone for a week or two; once we drove all the way across the country, camping along the way.

These were magical times for my family to enjoy the wonder and beauty of creation and to make memories together. Away from the prying eyes of parishioners and the responsibilities of being the minister's family, we were able to focus on our relationships with one another and on our shared experiences.

I am not sure how many actual memories my kids have of those camping experiences. Whenever we look at the camping slides, they are full of questions about where we were, how old they were, and what we did. In many cases, it is my job as mom to supply the details—or at least the ones I can still remember.

Nevertheless, what my children do remember is that they grew up in a family that went camping together and that valued the time away. They remember encounters with creation and deepened relationships. While they cannot recall all of the details, they remember that their childhood was blessed by those special times. Camping experiences helped to shape their lives, and they are more rich as adults because of those times we spent together.

Organized Camping

After years of camping as a family in the Northwest, we moved to the East Coast. It was there during seminary and afterward that I began my ministry as a church camp professional. As a camp director, I was privileged through the years to share what my family had loved about camping with campers, staff members, and retreat guests. Now as a developer of resources for families and camps, I continue to pass on to others the importance of temporary living in the outdoors.

When I moved to camp for the summer, my kids became campers—and later counselors—living in simple buildings, eating camp food, and participating in a wide variety of camp activities. They learned that the same skills—tolerance, cooperation, trust, listening—that had been necessary as our family camped were also needed as they lived with groups of kids their own age. The love of being outside and observing the rhythms of nature during family camping times enhanced their group camping times. Both of them were confident about their fire-building skills and flower-identifying abilities because they had grown up practicing them.

Why We Went Camping

Our family began camping for two reasons. The first was that my children's father grew up hiking and camping in the wild places around Seattle, Washington. A Boy Scout from early adolescence, he was a confident and able camp person. He brought to our family the love of—and comfort with—being outside close to the beauty and wonder of what God had made. The second major reason for our family camping was shortage of money. We simply could not afford hotel/Disneyland/cruise vacations. We used a small inheritance we received when the children were young to buy the camper. It paid us back many times over.

Camping also reflected our desire to live simply, to surround ourselves with the wonders of creation, and to escape from the requirements of the everyday. Although our choice was a pop-up camper rather than a tent—a compromise between my cottage vacations and E's backpacking—we had to live with only what we could pack in the camper and car.

Moreover, we wanted to expose our kids to the beautiful and historical places that surrounded our Northwest home. Camping trips often included a visit to a national park. We hid in our car when bears ventured into our picnic area during a trip to Mount Rainier, stood in awe in the canyons of Bryce, and wandered among the mountain laurel on the hillsides of the Cascades. Finally, getting away in our pop-up enabled us to escape from the roles of pastor and his family as well as the constant scrutiny of a small town. During camping trips we became just a regular family having fun together.

I wish we had had a book like this for our family camping trips for several reasons. We stood by lakes, awed by the reflection of snow-topped mountains; we watched a bear mosey by our campsite and off into the woods; we ran through the cold waves of the Pacific and cried out as our toes lost all feeling. God was there with us; a devotional book would have helped us to remember the presence of God.

Also, both Andrew and Sara grew up with a love of the outdoors and a desire to protect and preserve the environment. However, they have few skills for connecting their faith to their desire to care for creation. A book like this would have helped pave the road for such an understanding.

We often curled up together on the couch of our little home away from home to read stories and to sip hot cocoa. How wonderful it would have been to tell stories about God and to talk together about those stories and our shared experiences.

And finally, I wish we had had a book like this for our family camping trips because it would have helped us as parents to initiate creative expression and would have given us ideas for things we could do together. The kids' creativity emerged in all kinds of interesting ways. Sticks found along the beach became ponies; folded paper became boats for a meadow stream; long grasses became whistles. Planned activities and crafts would have further expanded their creativity.

My family was blessed by the times we spent together out-of-doors both camping as a family and at organized camps. My prayer is that you, too, will be blessed by times together outdoors—whether you are a family camping together or a leader working with a group of campers. I hope that you will discover anew the grace and love of our Creator God, who flung into being this wonderful and amazing world we call home.

May your heart and the hearts of those with whom you camp be filled with awe at what God has done and is doing in creation. I pray that you and your family group will leave your time of camping filled with a desire and commitment to care for and protect for future families this incredible place God has entrusted to us.

S'more Time!

S'mores are sweet treats made over a campfire with marshmallows, milk chocolate, and graham crackers. They are the perfect way to complete a day outdoors at camp. They are so good that you always want s'more!

Here's how to make them. You will need some green sticks or skewers, graham crackers, large marshmallows, and thin chocolate bars, such as Hershey's Milk Chocolate.

1. Build a campfire and let it burn down to hot coals.
2. Pass out green sticks or long skewers. Be sure they are 20–24 inches long so there won't be any burned fingers.
3. Give everyone one or two marshmallows to roast on the end of the stick or skewer. Be sure to skewer the middle of the marshmallows so they won't fall off into the fire.
4. While some are roasting the marshmallows, arrange the other ingredients. Break the graham crackers in half and place 2–4 squares of chocolate on the bottom half. Save the other graham cracker halves for the top of the S'mores.
5. When the marshmallows are toasty brown, place 1–2 marshmallows on top of each chocolate-graham cracker layer, and use the second half of the graham cracker to pull the marshmallows off the stick.
6. Press the second half on top of the marshmallow slightly to smash the ingredients together into a gooey sandwich called a S'more!

Like S'mores, time with God can be a perfect way to complete the fun of a day at camp. This book offers some creative ideas for how to cultivate such time with your family or group. I pray that when you are finished, you will want s'more!

For more kid-friendly camping recipes, including some fun variations on the classic S'mores, turn to pages 111–115.

How to Use This Book

The purpose of this book is to guide family groups in activities they can do together outdoors, to tell biblical stories in a way that is accessible to children, and to help family groups reflect on the connection between the biblical story and the experience they just shared. I use the title "family groups" with intention, because the devotions in this book can be used both by nuclear families going camping as well as by cabin groups within organized summer camps.

The devotions are intended for use with older preschool and elementary-aged children. Children in this age group are interested in all kinds of things in nature and still enjoy doing activities as a family group. The stories and the activities are created to appeal to their physical, spiritual, and cognitive skills. They are excited about discovering and trying out new things. Their imaginations are active and playful. Therefore, the activities are designed to engage their interests on many levels.

The devotional material is separated into five collections of biblical passages of seven days each. They provide a complete week of devotionals for use by a family during a camping trip or by a group of campers at a summer church camp. Each week of devotionals is organized around a biblical theme or group of stories.

God Creates

Day 1 (Genesis 1:1-5)
Day 2 (Genesis 1:6-8)
Day 3 (Genesis 1:9-13)
Day 4 (Genesis 1:14-19)
Day 5 (Genesis 1:20-23)
Day 6 (Genesis 1:24-31)
Day 7 (Genesis 2:1-3)

The Promise and the Wilderness

God's Call (Genesis 12:1-8; 21:1-3)
Holy Place (Genesis 28:10-11, 13, 15-19a)
The Burning Bush (Exodus 3:1-12)
Tent of Meeting (Exodus 33:7-10)
Food in the Wilderness (Exodus 16:1-6)
Resting and Remembering (Exodus 20:8-11)
God Gives the Good Land (Deuteronomy 8:7-10)

Songs and Prayers of Israel

Praise the Lord (Psalm 136:1-9)
Sing a New Song (Psalm 98:1a, 4-9)
God Cares for Creatures (Psalm 104:10-18, 21-22, 24)
Who Are Humans? (Psalm 8:1, 3-9)
Sheep and Shepherds (Psalm 23)
I Am a Green Tree (Psalm 52:8-9)
The Lord Has Made This Day (Psalm 118:1, 24, 27-29)

Following Jesus

Saying Thanks (Luke 17:11-18)
A Boy and His Lunch (John 6:1-14)
Lilies and Birds (Matthew 6:25-32)
Jesus Blesses the Children (Matthew 19:13-15)
Storm on the Lake (Mark 4:35-41)
Seaside Cookout (John 21:1-12)
The Little Man and the Tree (Luke 19:1-10)

Stories Jesus Told

Parable of the Vineyard (Matthew 20:1-16)
Parable of the Sower (Matthew 13:1-9)
Parable of Small Things (Luke 13:18-19)
Parable of the Lost Sheep (Luke 15:3-7)
Parable of the Rich Fool (Luke 12:13-21)
Parable of the Talents (Matthew 25:14-30)
Parable of the Good Samaritan (Luke 10:25-37)

Each devotional has six components: Theme, Claim the Time, A Way to Begin, Something to Do, Bible Discovery, and Prayer.

- *Theme* describes in a few words the thematic focus of the day's discussion.

- *Claim the Time* suggests a song or Bible verse you can use to signal the beginning of family time with God. Like a call to worship at the beginning of a church service, this song or verse, repeated every day, gathers your family group together and readies them for a time of focusing on God and creation.

- *A Way to Begin* provides one or two questions or discussion ideas to use before the "Something to Do" activity.

- *Something to Do* suggests an activity for a family group to engage in together. The activity, which connects to the biblical lesson that follows, is best done outside. Placing the activity before the lesson recognizes the developmental need of children for action and discovery. In this way, they can do the action and then reflect on it as they hear the biblical story and connect it to something real in their lives.

- *Bible Discovery* includes a retelling of the biblical passage. You are encouraged to read the Scripture passage in advance and then retell it to the children in your own words. Alternatively, you might involve older children or teens in the family group by asking them to read the passage aloud from a contemporary paraphrase of the Bible, such as Eugene Peterson's

The Message, the New Living Translation, or the Contemporary English Version. Why a retelling or biblical paraphrase? Long before the stories of the Bible were written down, they were told out loud—and in the days before electricity, the stories were often shared around a campfire. You can pass these stories on to your children in the same time-honored way the ancients did. Children can play a part in telling the stories too. Some suggestions for telling stories can be found later in this section.

- *Prayer* suggests a brief prayer that family groups can say together. However, the printed prayers are only a starting place for prayers that you can make together. Some suggestions for creating family prayers can be found later in this section.

Preceding each unit of devotionals, there is an introduction to the week's theme and group of biblical stories, as well as a list of supplies you will need for theme-related activities. The introduction offers basic background material for parents or adult leaders. For the most part, this information is not essential to the use of the devotions but may equip you to answer children's questions about the setting of the biblical stories.

The supplies needed for any week are minimal. However, they may include items you would not normally take on a camping trip. Read the list over before you leave home so that you will be sure to have everything required. You may also want to create a craft box as part of your regular camping supplies. Include such items as glue, scissors, crayons, markers, painting supplies, construction paper, and plain paper.

Where and When to Use the Devotionals

These devotionals are intended for use outdoors. Most of them call for interaction with nature. Many of them invite family groups to take a walk around the campsite or to explore some aspect of creation hands-on. You are encouraged to choose a space near your cabin, tent, or camper to begin each day and then to move around as suggested in the activity. A bench, table, or blanket located away from the distractions of other people will provide a quiet place to hear the biblical story.

You can decide the best time to set aside during the day for your devotional. After breakfast or after dinner are times often chosen by family groups. However, you may choose any time of day that works for you. The time might vary with your schedule and the other activities you have planned for the day. The devotion itself may also determine the time, such as a breakfast cookout, a night hike, or a picnic lunch.

You may want to separate the times you do Something to Do and Bible Discovery and do them at two different times during the day. For example, you may want to do the Something to Do first thing in the morning and then consider the Bible Discovery during quiet time in the afternoon.

One of the challenges of doing things with children outside is the constant distraction built into the natural setting. Insects, toads, poison ivy, a bird overhead, a rustling in the grass or trees nearby—these are just a few of the things that will capture the attention of a young person. Although you may be tempted to go inside to escape these distractions, consider turning the interruption into an opportunity to talk about how that distraction is a part of God's creation. Ask the children why God included it in creation.

Telling Bible Stories

1. Puppets

There are a variety of ways children can make puppets to act out the story, either as you tell it or after you have heard it together.

- *Finger puppets.* Put a bandage over the top of a finger and draw a face on the bandage.

- *Paper plate puppets.* Draw a face on the eating surface of the paper plate. Attach a craft stick to the back with tape.

- *Clothespin puppets.* Hold the clothespin up as if you were going to push it onto a clothesline, and draw on a face. Use napkins or bandanas to "dress" the puppet.

2. Drama

Introduce children to these easy ways to do drama. Encourage them to create their own skits based on the biblical story.

- *Skit.* After reading or retelling the story, act it out with children and adults playing different roles and speaking memorized or improvised lines.

- *Tableau.* Make a list of the scenes in the story. Then have the children freeze in a pose to represent each scene as the story is read or retold aloud.

- *Pantomime.* Have one person narrate the story. The participants act it out silently as the narrator describes what the characters are doing.

- *Media interview.* Take turns being interviewer and interviewees. Make a list of questions to ask the main Bible characters about what they saw and heard.

3. Artistic Response

Children of all ages will enjoy the opportunity to use their imaginations to create a written or visual response to the story or theme of the devotion.

- *Mural.* Have everyone draw or paint a picture of the various scenes in the story. (Use the craft supplies recommended on page 4). Tape the drawings together to create a mural that tells the story. Hang it on the wall of your tent, cabin, or camper—and display it at home.

- *Comic strip.* Make a list of the scenes from the story, and draw cartoon panels of them on white paper, using pencils, crayons, or markers.

- *Song.* Write new words to a familiar tune or hymn melody, and retell the story as a song.

- *Poem.* Use one of the following poem forms to tell the story or highlight the biblical lesson.

Cinquain is based on a certain number of words in each of its five lines. The words can be any length and do not have to rhyme.

Line 1: One word—the subject of the poem (a person, place, or thing)

Line 2: Two words (adjectives) that describe the subject in line 1

Line 3: Three words (verb phrase) that depict the subject's action

Line 4: Four words that describe a feeling about the subject

Line 5: One word that renames the subject in line 1, a synonym in significance if not in literal meaning

EXAMPLE:

God
Compassionate, sovereign
Making everything new
Inspires my joyful hallelujah!
Creator

Haiku is a form of nonrhyming poetry from Japan. It has three lines of five, seven, and five syllables, traditionally invoking an aspect of nature or the seasons. Here's how you form a Haiku:

Line 1: Five syllables

Line 2: Seven syllables

Line 3: Five syllables

EXAMPLE:

The early morning
Colors creep from blush to blue
As dawn dazzling breaks

Creating Family Prayers

Here are a variety of ways family groups can make their own prayers of thanksgiving, praise, confession, or petition.

- *Litanies.* Make a list of what everyone in the family group enjoys or appreciates about God's creation. Read the items on the list one at a time, pausing for the rest of the group to respond with a simple sentence, such as: "Thank you, God, for all good things," or "Praise God, for God is wonderful."

- *Responsive readings.* Psalms were the prayers of Israel. Either read through a psalm as a litany, with other members responding with a simple sentence, or have everyone take turns reading a verse and pray through the psalm together.

- *Prayer circle.* Stand or sit in a circle. Have each person speak the name of the person on his or her right. Pause a moment for silent or spoken prayers for that person. Continue around the circle until every person's name has been spoken and prayed for.

- *Popcorn prayers.* During prayer time group members can "pop up" with a prayer when they have something to say. Participants pray in no particular order.

- *Squeeze prayer.* Sit or stand in a circle holding hands. One person opens the prayer time, and prayer continues around the circle. Anyone who doesn't want to pray out loud may squeeze the hand of the next person, and the prayer is passed on without awkward delay or unnecessary embarrassment to shy members.

- *Praying stick.* A "talking stick" is offered to anyone in the family group who wants to pray. Only the person holding the stick may speak, and only those who request the stick are expected to pray.

Remember: This devotional book offers you, your children, and God a chance to have fun together. So often we limit our interactions with God to occasions when we have to wear good clothes, talk quietly, and sit primly indoors. Camp experiences help us get another view of God—a view of our Creator who is full of imagination and whimsy! (This should be clear to us whenever we look at the some of the creatures God has made. Only a God with a sense of fun would have made a giraffe or zebra or ostrich!)

Help your children to engage with this loving God who made the amazing world of nature. Guide them to use their senses to explore God's wonders. God intends for all of us to enjoy creation. Seize this opportunity for you and your children to rejoice in the vast goodness God has made for you and all people.

Introduction

Tents and camping go hand in hand. Whether the tent is a fully equipped RV, a wall tent, or a fly tarp strung across a rope, there remains the close association between the idea of camping and the image of the tent. That image speaks to us of the outdoors, of flexibility, and of simplicity.

Temporary living is an image found in Scripture. We are descendants of tent dwellers who followed their sheep and goats to green grass and fresh water. Our Old Testament ancestors, while they would not have called themselves campers, also lived in tents. In the early days before their slavery in Egypt, the Hebrews lived in tents and traveled from place to place with their flocks. During the forty years in the wilderness, the Israelites moved their tents along the journey toward the land of God's promise.

Those migratory people, wanting to understand the presence of God with them in their journey, also erected a "tent of meeting" where God could dwell. The book of Exodus first portrays this tabernacle as a tent pitched by Moses outside the camp, at a distance from the people (33:7-11). Subsequently, God gives elaborate instructions for a larger structure with rich decoration and the best craftsmanship of the people (see Exodus 35–40), which eventually came to be erected in the center of the camp, in the midst of the tribal groupings (see Numbers 2). When Moses crossed the threshold of this tent, God's presence came as a pillar of smoke, surrounded the tent, and entered it. Wherever Israel camped, God was there with them.

In the same way, we can expect God to be present with us as we camp. God will dwell within the "tent of meeting" we create. God will be present with us as we explore the wonders of creation, listen to each other's words, and find meaning in the stories of God's people.

Camping experiences offer a unique opportunity for our faith to grow. Faith in the creator God will expand as we watch the changing color of the sky at sunset or listen to the morning song of birds or taste blackberries picked fresh from the bush. Our hearts will fill with awe and thanksgiving in the goodness of what God has made. The ordinary events of a camping experience become a chance to stop and say, "God is here."

Our faith will grow as we take time together to listen to the stories of God's people from Scripture. For many centuries, before these stories were written down, they were told as family groups gathered around campfires at the end of the day. Parents and grandparents told the children about what God had done. Camping gives us a chance as adults to sit around the fire and pass along these biblical stories to our children.

Our faith will grow as God's love becomes incarnate in the love and closeness found within everyday life as a family group. As humans we cannot cross over into the sacred without the help of things we can touch and see, taste and feel. We need tangible signs to enable our experience of that which is holy, that which is "set apart." Living simply together outside gives us time to notice that which is holy.

Why Go Camping?

Think for a moment about the reasons you go camping. What is it you want for your children and for your family as a whole? There are no right or wrong reasons, but I expect there are some common purposes and values that bind together all those who choose to go camping or to send their kids to camp.

First, we desire to slow down and step away from our hectic lives. We long to stop the constant rush and bedlam of keeping up with everyone's schedules and needs. Camping—whether in a tent, cabin, or RV—offers the opportunity to go someplace else and to spend days free of deadlines.

Second, we desire to live more simply. Camping—regardless of the form, requires us to set priorities. We have to decide what we absolutely need and what we can leave behind. Depending on the level of camping, the choices may be easier in some cases. Obviously, a backpacking trip sets the most limits on our choices, since everything we need has to be carried on our backs. A family's decision about how to camp also determines the level of human comforts and technology they can take along. Regardless of the type of camping, it always necessitates taking fewer possessions than we have at home.

Third, we desire to nurture the relationships between family members that often get neglected in the rush of demanding schedules. Camping has an entirely different emphasis than amusement park vacations. Places like Disneyland invite us to stay in an amusement mind-set—someone else does something to entertain us, occupy our attention, and keep us busy—but camping family groups decide what they will do together with their time without the constant distraction of an entertainment-based stimulus.

Finally, we desire to interact with God's creation. It is impossible—even in a mega RV—to totally ignore what is outside the windows or tent flap. Closeness to nature and camping are inseparable. The choice to go camping is almost identical to the choice to be outside in nature. How much engagement with nature you have depends on the level of camping. A stay at a mountain lake and a stay at an RV park offer different things, but both reflect a desire to enjoy some exposure to creation. Otherwise, we would have gone to a hotel!

Camping, the Creation, and You

This is a book for family groups who love being outside in the beauty of God's creation together. One thing is clear and consistent throughout Scripture: God created the world and all its plants and creatures, and God called it good. Also apparent in the stories of Creation is God's intention for humans to nurture and care for the creation on behalf of and in partnership with God. Genesis 1 says that God gave humans dominion, meaning that we can make decisions about how to protect and conserve what God has given to us (v. 26). Genesis 2 tells us that God instructed human beings to care for and till the garden God made (v. 15).

Global warming, destruction of habitats, and damage to ecosystems are all signs that humans haven't done very well at following God's instructions and invitation to care for the creation. Our human tendency is to use the resources of the earth to benefit our own wealth or our own comfort. Each of us needs to ask two questions of ourselves: How have I failed to care for creation? In what way have my choices contributed to the damage?

This is a book for families who are concerned about the care, conservation, and preservation of creation. We do not have to stay stuck in our old ways. Nature itself reminds us about the power of renewal. While death is a reality in the natural order, new life always appears out of death. Compost—the earth's leftovers—refreshes the soil, rain swells dry riverbeds, and new growth appears out of dead stumps. The process of renewal goes on and on. It is a reminder to us that each new day gives us the chance to make different choices.

A sequence of steps can move our children and us from just thinking about creation care to making concrete decisions about actions we can take. The first step is to pay attention. We do that through using our senses to look for colors, patterns, variation, sounds, and changes in the environment. Second, as we do this we are filled with awe and thanksgiving and amazement for what God has done. Finally, we will be moved to ask what we can do to conserve and protect this extraordinary world God has made. Our choices can be simple or complex, big or small, but each of them makes a difference.

This is a book for families who want to take stories of God with them on camping trips. The Old and the New Testament peoples lived in a world very different than ours. They were directly connected to nature and its rhythms. They grew their own food, interacted with creatures both wild and domesticated, got up with the sun and went to bed with the coming of darkness, and organized their religious celebrations around the seasons. Most stories in Scripture reflect the outdoor settings and lifestyles of the biblical peoples.

Reading the stories of the Bible while camping together helps us feel closer to its people and the way they lived. Jesus sat outside to teach; he went fishing with his followers; he walked along dusty roads to get from one place to another. We do not know for sure, but many think that he and the disciples camped at night, cooking over a fire and sleeping under the stars. Our camp time allows us the opportunity to hear biblical stories in a natural setting and gives us time to reflect together on the meaning of those stories.

This is a book for families who want to decide on specific actions they can take when they get home. As noted above, the choice to go camping in the first place reflects a desire to be outside in nature and to follow some different rhythms. Camping also gives us the opportunity to engage intentionally in observing and exploring the ecosystems near us and to find wonder in what God has made. That intentional attention can move us to translate our wonder into specific actions we can take at home to care for and protect creation. Deciding to act is the first step, and choosing an action is a second step.

God Creates

The Seven Days of Genesis 1–2:3

Introduction

"In the beginning God. . . ." These familiar words begin the book of Genesis; they begin the Old Testament; they begin the Bible. As we continue reading in that first chapter of the Bible, we hear the story of God's creation of the whole world in six days and how God rested on the seventh day.

You may find it helpful as you read through the Scripture passages this week to know something about the people who first told the stories and later wrote them down. They did not possess the scientific skills or understanding that we have today. What they had was a deep faith that the God who was revealed to them through the covenant and the Law was also the God of creation.

Keep in mind that Israel was surrounded by cultures that believed in many gods—each of these gods was responsible for one aspect of creation and of the lives of the people. So for the Hebrews to put their faith in one single God who both related to them in their everyday lives and created everything was a radical stance to take.

When the Hebrews first told the story of God's creation of the world as they knew it, theirs was a song of faith. They were declaring that their God was the only god who created; their God was in a special relationship with them. They were unique among all the other peoples.

We know that we live on a round globe lighted by one among millions of stars. We have walked on the moon, traveled to the bottom of the ocean, and unlocked the structure of atoms and DNA. Our worldview takes all this for granted. The ancient peoples, however, did not have our scientific knowledge. Their worldview was created by their limited experience. They knew about the sun and the night sky, about the importance of rivers for the growth of plants in dry land, and about the creatures that lived in their environment. Their worldview was framed by what they could observe and the places they could travel. As we read their words from Genesis, we must come with an understanding and a picture in our minds of that view of the reality.

The ancients believed that the earth was a flat platform supported on tall pilings over a deep sea. Above the sea and the dry land was a huge dome—picture the ones we find over football stadiums. The dome held out the waters above the earth, and openings in the dome let in the rain. As strange as all that may be to us, it was the way they viewed the world.

As you read the stories of each day of creation with your children this week, you can help your children understand that these words in Genesis 1 are a song of praise to the one God who created everything. Instill in them a sense of the goodness of all that God created and God's call to both ancient peoples and to us to preserve and protect these gifts of God.

Following the account of creation each day, your family group can make a picture of that day. Each person can work individually on the picture, or you can create a single picture together. At the end of the week, you will have an illustrated account of creation.

Supplies You Will Need This Week

Drawing paper, construction paper, or paper plates
Markers, crayons, or pastels
Large pan or bowl for water if there is no natural body
   of water near the campsite
Field guides for local plants and birds
Large towel or tarp for watching the night sky
Constellation map (optional)
Bibles

Day 1
Genesis 1:1-5
THEME: *Light and dark*

Claim the Time

As a signal for the beginning of devotional time, sing a simple song, such as "Awesome God," or one verse of "All Things Bright and Beautiful." Or you can say, "On the first day of creation, God saw what he had done and said it was very good."

A Way to Begin

Invite all group members to name something they like about the light and about the dark. Ask them to tell about things they like to do when it is light and things they like to do when it is dark.

Something to Do

Today plan to take two walks, one when the sun is out (remember that even if it is raining or overcast, the sun is out) and one after dark. Choose a place at the campsite that is away from people and buildings. In the daylight at that chosen place, invite group members to notice what they can see in the light. When you come back after dark, encourage them to think about the differences they notice. Remind them both times that God made both light and dark and called them good. During each walk you can ask questions such as the following:

- What colors do you notice? How far into the shadowy places can you see?
- How do you feel when it is light and you can see things?
- How do you feel when it is dark and you can't see things around you?

Bible Discovery

Introduce the first chapter of the Bible. Explain that this chapter of Genesis tells the story of God's creation of the world in six days. Tell everyone that during the week you will be reading about what God made each day. Explain that today is the story of the first day of creation.

When God began to create, there was nothing. The world was dark and empty. Imagine what that would be like. Then a wind began to blow. What do you think that sounded like? The wind was the Spirit of God. The Spirit blew through the air and over the dark waters. The Spirit blew over the empty world. Then God looked around at all the darkness and said, "Let there be light." Imagine what it would be like when there was light for the very first time. Right then in the world God was creating, there was darkness and there was light. God decided to give the light the name day; and the darkness he decided to call night. God looked around at the light and the dark and saw that it was good.

Say all together: "There was evening, and there was morning—the first day."

As individuals or a family group, use crayons, markers, or paints to draw the first day of creation on paper or paper plates. At the end of the week, you will have an illustrated story of creation.

Prayer (Together)

You can use the words of this prayer, or see Creating Family Prayers on page 10.

God of the day and of the night, thank you for both light and darkness. Help me to remember every morning that you made the day. Amen.

Day 2

Genesis 1:6-8

THEME: *Water*

Claim the Time

As a signal for the beginning of devotional time, sing a simple song, such as "Awesome God," or one verse of "All Things Bright and Beautiful." Or you can say, "On the second day of creation, God saw what he had done and said it was very good."

A Way to Begin

Invite group members to say something they like about water. Ask them to make a list of all the things they can do with water, such as drink it, wash in it, and swim in it.

Something to Do

Walk to some water near the campsite or fill up a large bowl or pan with water. If you are going to walk in the water, you may want to wear water shoes. Encourage group members to look for creatures living in the water and to see what plants are growing in the water or along the shoreline. Ask them to think about what their lives would be like without water. Sit by the water and have some water to drink. Explain that some people don't have fresh water to drink. As you are sitting by the water, you can ask questions such as the following:

- What do you like best about water?
- If you could have only three buckets of water a day, what would you do with each bucketful?
- How can we be more careful of the fresh water we use during our time at the campsite and after we go home?

Bible Discovery

Introduce the next section of the creation story. Explain to group members that today they will be hearing about the second day of creation.

When God continued to make creation, there was lots of water all over and under the heavens. There wasn't any land. So God put a big dome over the waters—just like the dome over a big football stadium. The dome kept the water out of that space, so underneath was dry. God gave the dome a name—sky.

Say all together: "There was evening, and there was morning—the second day."

As individuals or a family group, use crayons, markers or paints to draw the second day of creation on paper or paper plates. At the end of the week, you will have an illustrated story of creation.

Prayer (Together)

You can use the words of this prayer, or see Creating Family Prayers on page 10.

God of the heavens and the waters, thank you for blue skies and water. Help me to remember to enjoy them every day. Amen.

Day 3

Genesis 1:9-13

THEME: *Seeds*

Claim the Time

As a signal for the beginning of devotional time, sing a simple song, such as "Awesome God," or one verse of "All Things Bright and Beautiful." Or you can say, "On the third day of creation, God saw what he had done and said it was very good."

A Way to Begin

Invite group members to name all the things they like that grow from seeds. Encourage them to tell what their favorite food is that grows from a plant.

Something to Do

Walk to some places where a lot of different plants and trees are growing. If you have a field guide for local plants, take it along. Stop along the way and look carefully at plants and trees. Have group members choose two or three they want to look at. Have them see if they can find out where the seed is for the plant or tree. You can use the field guide to identify the plant and see a picture of the seed. At the end of the walk, ask everyone what would happen if there were no seeds left in the world. As you are walking, you can ask questions such as the following:

- What are some plants that don't grow from seeds?
- What do you think is most amazing about seeds?
- What are some different ways that seeds move from place to place?

Bible Discovery

Introduce the next section of the creation story. Explain to group members that today they will be hearing about the third day of creation.

God now looked at the dry land under the dome and called the dry land earth. Where the waters were gathered up, God gave them the name oceans. And God saw the earth and the oceans and said that they were very good. There was nothing growing on the earth, so God created plants. There were flowers with seeds and grains and vegetable plants and poison ivy and grapevines. (You can name some other plants that God made on the third day.) Then God made fruit trees. God made apple trees and pecan trees and cherry trees and fig trees. And fruit was growing on the trees, with seeds inside to grow more trees just like them. (You can name some other kinds of trees that God made on the third day.) God looked around at all the green plants and trees and said that all of them were very good.

Say all together: "There was evening, and there was morning—the third day."

As individuals or a family group, use crayons, markers, or paints to draw the third day of creation on paper or paper plates. At the end of the week, you will have an illustrated story of creation.

Prayer (Together)

You can use the words of this prayer, or see Creating Family Prayers on page 10.

God of earth, thank you for all the colors and smells and tastes of what you have made. Help me to remember to stop and taste and smell and see your creation every day. Amen.

Day 4
Genesis 1:14-19
THEME: *Lights in the night sky*

Claim the Time

As a signal for the beginning of devotional time, sing a simple song, such as "Awesome God," or one verse of "All Things Bright and Beautiful." Or you can say, "On the fourth day of creation, God saw what he had done and said it was very good."

A Way to Begin

Invite group members to tell what they like best about being outside at night. Ask them what they know about the stars.

Something to Do

After dark, go to a flat, open place away from the reflection of lights from the campsite or nearby town. Put down tarps or large towels and turn off the flashlights. Have group members lie down and look up at the stars. Encourage them to look at all the stars and tell what they notice. Tell them that ancient peoples saw pictures in the sky. Look at a constellation map if you have one, and try to find the constellations. Talk about how you feel when you look at the night sky. As you are looking at the sky, you can ask questions such as the following:

- Which stars look bigger or closer than the others?
- What pictures can you make by connecting the stars?
- How do you think God is close to you when you look at the stars?

Bible Discovery

Introduce the next section of the creation story. Explain to group members that today they will be hearing about the fourth day of creation.

So far God had created light and dark, a dome and water, dry land and oceans, and all kinds of plants and trees with fruit and seeds. Now God put lights in the dome. They are the stars that we see at night. God made two great lights, the moon for nighttime and the sun for daytime. The sun and the moon helped to make day and night, winter and summer, autumn and spring—the cycle of the seasons made up months and years. And God saw that it was good.

Say all together: "There was evening, and there was morning— the fourth day."

As individuals or a family group, use crayons, markers, or paints to draw the fourth day of creation on paper or paper plates. At the end of the week, you will have an illustrated story of creation.

Prayer (Together)

You can use the words of this prayer, or see Creating Family Prayers *on page 10.*

God of the sun, moon, and stars, thank you for their bright lights. Help me to stop and look at the stars and enjoy the warmth of the sun every day. Amen.

Day 5

Genesis 1:20-23

THEME: *Birds and Fish*

Claim the Time

As a signal for the beginning of devotional time, sing a simple song, such as "Awesome God," or one verse of "All Things Bright and Beautiful." Or you can say, "On the fifth day of creation, God saw what he had done and said it was very good."

A Way to Begin

Invite group members to say something they like about birds. Ask them to name as many birds as they can. You might want to record the list of birds.

Something to Do

Walk to several habitats near the campsite. At each habitat, listen for birds. Look around and see if you can match the sounds you hear to the birds making them. Move very slowly so you won't startle them. Use the field guides to identify them and to find out what they eat and where they live. Check the list you made earlier to see how many of the birds on the list you spotted during your walk and how many additional ones you saw. Invite everyone to think about what it would be like to be a bird flying over the land. As you are walking, looking, and listening, ask questions such as the following:

- Why do you think birds have "songs"?
- What do you think it would be like to be a bird?
- How would things look from above the earth?

Bible Discovery

Introduce the next section of the creation story. Explain to group members that today they will be hearing about the fifth day of creation.

Remember that on the third day, God made plants and trees with fruit and seeds on the earth; and God made oceans surrounding the land. Now God wanted to fill the oceans and sky with animals, so God made swarms of living things to swim around in the oceans and birds to fly above the earth. God also made great sea monsters to live in the oceans. (You can name some of the fish that swim in the oceans and birds that fly in the sky.) God saw that all the creatures were very good. God blessed them all and told them to have babies so the oceans would be filled with fish and the sky would be filled with birds.

Say all together: "There was evening, and there was morning— the fifth day."

As individuals or a family group, use crayons, markers, or paints to draw the fifth day of creation on paper or paper plates. At the end of the week, you will have an illustrated story of creation.

Prayer (Together)

You can use the words of this prayer, or see Creating Family Prayers on page 10.

God of the birds and fish and sea monsters and every living thing, thank you for making so many interesting animals! Help me to be careful of their food and homes every day. Amen.

Day 6

Genesis 1:24-31
THEME: *Creatures*

Claim the Time

As a signal for the beginning of devotional time, sing a simple song, such as "Awesome God," or one verse of "All Things Bright and Beautiful." Or you can say, "On the sixth day of creation, God saw what he had done and said it was very good."

A Way to Begin

Invite group members to name the creatures that live at or near the campsite. They may have to listen for some of the creatures. Remind them that the animals may be domesticated or wild.

Something to Do

To find out what animals live near your campsite, take a walk to look for signs of the animals, such as footprints, and the animals themselves. You can interview other people at the campsite to find out what animals they have seen or know about. Think about the things animals need to have for food and a safe place to live. Encourage everyone to look around and see things near the campsite that might hurt or endanger the animals, such as a highway nearby, new buildings, or trash where they can get it. As you are finding out about the animals, you can ask questions such as the following:

- What kind of animal that lives near the campsite do you like best?
- What are some things near the campsite that could harm that animal?
- What is one way you can protect that animal from that danger?

Bible Discovery

Introduce the next section of the creation story. Explain to group members that today they will be hearing about the sixth day of creation.

On the morning of the sixth day, God created all land creatures—cattle and creeping things and wild animals. Imagine all the creatures God made. Think about how different they all are. God looked at what he had made and decided it was very good. Then God decided to make humans. God made them in the image of God to be like God. God blessed the humans—that is, God wished them to have good things. God told them to have lots of babies and to be like good rulers to the rest of creation. God gave them the plants, the trees with seeds, the wild animals, the birds and fish, and the creeping things, and said to take good care of them. And God saw that everything was very good.

Say all together: "There was evening, and there was morning— the sixth day."

As individuals or a family group, use crayons, markers, or paints to draw the sixth day of creation on paper or paper plates. At the end of the week, you will have an illustrated story of creation.

Prayer (Together)

You can use the words of this prayer, or see Creating Family Prayers on page 10.

God of all people everywhere, thank you for making us all so different and for loving us. Help me to remember every day that I am your precious child. Amen.

Day 7

Genesis 2:1-3

THEME: *Rest*

Claim the Time

As a signal for the beginning of devotional time, sing a simple song, such as "Awesome God," or one verse of "All Things Bright and Beautiful." Or you can say, "On the seventh day of creation, God saw what he had done and said it was very good."

A Way to Begin

Invite group members to tell something they like to do when they are resting. Ask them to name some of the reasons it is important to rest.

Something to Do

Remind everyone that animals and plants rest. Talk about animals that hibernate and plants that are dormant during the winter. Plan a way that the family group can rest together. Take a blanket and some snacks to a place at the campsite that you like and decide how long you will rest there. Talk about your favorite things about being at camp, and brainstorm together things you can do after you go home to take care of God's creation. Write a prayer thanking God for everyone's favorite things in creation, or read the whole Genesis 1 account of the creation using the illustrations you made each day. As you are resting, you can ask questions such as the following:

- What was your favorite day of creation during the week?
- What do you think is the most wonderful thing God created?
- How will you take care of creation when you go home?

Bible Discovery

Introduce the next section of the creation story. Explain to group members that today they will be hearing about the seventh day of creation.

For six days God worked really hard on creation. Remember all the things that God made. God created the earth and all its creatures and fish and birds. God made plants for them to eat and gave them water to swim in. God made the heavens and the land, the sun, moon, and stars. And at last God created human beings and asked them to take care of everything that God had made. Every day God declared that what he had made was good. Imagine how God felt after six days of creating. Now that creation was all finished, God decided to rest. So that is exactly what God did. God rested, and God blessed that rest and called it holy. Later on in the Bible, God made a rule for all God's people to rest on the seventh day too. God called it the Sabbath.

Say all together: "On the seventh day, God rested from all the work he had done in creation."

As individuals or a family group, use crayons, markers, or paints to draw the seventh day of creation on paper or paper plates. Line up the days of creation to make your illustrated story.

Prayer (Together)

You can use the words of this prayer, or see Creating Family Prayers on page 10.

God of the Sabbath, forgive us when we don't stop to rest but keep going and going and going. Help me to slow down every day and to remember how wonderful all of your creation is. Amen.

The Promise and the Wilderness

Passages from Genesis, Exodus, and Deuteronomy

Introduction

Our ancestors in the Christian faith were nomads. They were herders who followed their flocks of sheep and goats to places where the animals could eat grass and drink fresh water. Their homes were tents so they could move around as they led the flocks.

The Israelites were just one tribe or family group among all the other nomads who lived in the lands of the Middle East—now Iraq, Iran, Jordan, and Israel—in ancient times. However, one thing made them unique among all the tribes—their belief in a single God. Their neighbors believed in a lot of little gods; Israel believed in only one—the God of creation and covenant.

God chose Israel to be God's people and entered into a covenant relationship with them. The terms of the covenant—a reciprocal agreement between two parties—were clear: "I will be your God, and you will be my people." God would sustain, protect, and love the people of Israel; the people of Israel would worship only this one God and follow the commandments that God gave to them.

The Old Testament tells us the story of God's covenant people as they attempted to be faithful to God and to keep their part of

35

the promise. Even though the people of Israel broke the laws God gave them, God was always faithful to them, watching over Israel and protecting them from their enemies.

We read in Genesis about God's promise to Abraham to make him the father of a great nation of people and to give his heirs a land of their own "flowing with milk and honey." The first five books of the Bible give us the record of Israel's circuitous journey to the Promised Land, passing through slavery in Egypt and wandering for forty years in the wilderness.

For a long time, these stories were not written down but were told orally. At the end of the day, God's people gathered around the campfire to hear stories about God. They told of God's greatness and faithfulness.

As you camp with your children this week, you are following in a long tradition of God's people who lived outside among the natural world and who worshiped the God of creation. They too gazed up at the starry heavens, watched the sun rise in the east, and drank deeply of cold water in the heat of the day.

Help your children to imagine what it must have been like to live such a nomadic life. Invite them to imagine what it would be like to be completely dependent on creation for all your food, clothing, and shelter; to sleep outside in a tent all year; and to trust God so completely that they would walk across the desert for forty years to reach the new home God had promised to them.

Try to tell the stories to your children instead of reading them. Engage your children with the people of the story and the God of creation. Help them to pay attention to the places where they feel God's presence with them.

Supplies You Will Need This Week

Construction paper
Markers
Bible Times Food (see list on page 47)
Bibles

God's Call

Genesis 12:1-8; 21:1-3

THEME: *Promises*

Claim the Time

As a signal for the beginning of devotional time, sing a simple song, such as "The Lord Is Good to Me," or one verse of "Great Is Thy Faithfulness." Or you can paraphrase a verse from a psalm, such as "We will tell the glorious deeds of the LORD and the wonders God has done" (Psalm 78:4).

A Way to Begin

Invite group members to tell about a promise they made or that someone made to them. Ask them whether the promise was kept or not. Invite them to tell how they felt when the promise was kept or broken. Tell them that during this week at the campsite they will have a chance to make promises about how they will care for the creation nearby.

Something to Do

Walk around the campsite and talk about ways everyone can care for creation, such as picking up trash, staying on paths, not breaking living branches, and not killing any creatures. After the walk, invite everyone to make a promise to do one of these things during the camp time. Write down the promises and post the list where group members can see it as a reminder of their promises. As you are walking around, you can ask questions such as the following:

- What are some ways we can damage the creation during our time at camp?
- How can we prevent doing damage to the creation?
- What is one way you can keep your promise during camp time?

Bible Discovery

Introduce today's story from the Old Testament. Explain that it tells how God called to Abraham and made a promise to him. Tell, read, or act out this story. Older children can read Genesis 12:1-3 from a contemporary version of the Bible.

Abraham and Sarah were very old and had no children. One day God came to Abraham and made him a promise. God told Abraham that he and Sarah would have a son and that through that son God would make a great nation of people. Even though Abraham had no idea how God would make such an impossible thing happen, he trusted God. Sarah and Abraham packed up all their belongings and traveled to the land of Canaan. When they got there, God told them that God would give this land to Abraham and Sarah's descendants. And not long afterward, Sarah and Abraham had a son and named him Isaac.

After you have heard the story, ask the following questions:

- What do you think Abraham said to Sarah after he heard God's promise?
- How do you think Abraham and Sarah felt when Isaac was born?
- What do you think of God's promise? What are some of God's other promises in the Bible?
- What are some ways to show our trust in God's promises here at camp and after we go home?

Prayer (Together)

You can use the words of this prayer, or see Creating Family Prayers on page 10.

Wonderful God, thank you for keeping your promises to Abraham and Sarah. Help me to trust you to keep your promises to me. Amen.

Holy Places

Genesis 28:10-11, 13, 15-19a

THEME: *Special place where God feels present*

Claim the Time

As a signal for the beginning of devotional time, sing a simple song, such as "The Lord Is Good to Me," or one verse of "Great Is Thy Faithfulness." Or you can paraphrase a verse from a psalm, such as "We will tell the glorious deeds of the LORD and the wonders God has done" (Psalm 78:4).

A Way to Begin

Invite group members to tell about a place where God seemed very close to them. Encourage them to tell how they felt having a sense of God's presence. Talk with your family group about the special places around the campsite where they have felt God's presence.

Something to Do

If your family group is unfamiliar with the campsite, take a walk around. Once you have chosen a place where you feel God's presence, decide a way to mark this as a holy place. You may want to build an altar or lay flowers or make a circle of rocks. Listen to today's story as you sit in your holy space. As you are creating the space, you can ask questions such as the following:

- How do you feel standing in this place?
- What makes this place special to you?
- How can we use this space this week as a place to worship God and be near God?

Bible Discovery

Introduce today's story from the Old Testament. Explain that it tells about a time when God came to Jacob in a dream. Tell, read, or act out this story. Older children can read Genesis 28:10-11, 13, 15-19a from a contemporary version of the Bible.

Esau and Jacob, the sons of Isaac, had a fight, and Jacob left home. One night out in the desert he was confused about what to do or where to go. He had no pillow, so he put a stone under his head, and while he was sleeping, he had a dream. God stood beside him and promised that he would give the land near where Jacob was sleeping to him and all his descendants. When Jacob woke up, he knew that the place was holy ground because God was there. He stood his pillow stone upright and poured oil on top of it. He called the place Bethel, which means "house of God." Later Jacob's many descendants came to live near Bethel in the good land God promised to him that night.

After hearing the story, ask questions such as the following:

- How do you think Jacob felt when he had to sleep alone in the desert with just a stone for his pillow?
- What do you think God looked like in the dream?
- If God came to you in a dream and made a promise, what is the first thing you would want to do in the morning?
- How do you know a place is holy?

Prayer (Together)

You can use the words of this prayer, or see Creating Family Prayers on page 10.

God of Abraham and Jacob, thank you for being present with Jacob when he was out in the desert. Help me to feel your presence when I am outside. Amen.

The Burning Bush

Exodus 3:1-12

THEME: *God's presence in nature*

Claim the Time

As a signal for the beginning of devotional time, sing a simple song, such as "The Lord Is Good to Me," or one verse of "Great Is Thy Faithfulness." Or you can paraphrase a verse from a psalm, such as "We will tell the glorious deeds of the LORD and the wonders God has done" (Psalm 78:4).

A Way to Begin

Invite the group members to think about a campfire and to describe something that happens when a fire burns. Ask them what happens to the wood in the fire. Encourage them to say something they like about campfires.

Something to Do

Arrange to build a campfire tonight. Be sure to check with the staff of the campsite to find out their rules about building fires. You can either plan to cook dinner over the fire or enjoy s'mores after dinner. During the day collect firewood and prepare the campfire site if you need to. Get a bucket of water to keep nearby and use it to put out the fire when you are finished. As you are watching the fire, explain that in today's story God does a really remarkable thing to get the attention of Moses. God starts a fire that does not burn up the tree. During your campfire you can ask questions such as the following:

- What do you love best about a campfire?
- What would you think if you saw a fire that was not burning the wood?
- What do you want to say to God right now?

Bible Discovery

Introduce today's story from the Old Testament. Explain that it is
about God's call to Moses to lead the Israelites out of slavery in
Egypt. Tell, read, or act out this story. Older children can read
Exodus 3:1-12 from a contemporary version of the Bible.

Jacob moved his family to Egypt when there was a famine in
Israel. After Jacob died, a new king ruled Egypt, and he forced all
of Jacob's family to become slaves. They had to work hard and
complained to God about being slaves. They wanted to go to the
land God had promised Abraham. One day Moses—one of
Israelites—was out herding his sheep. He looked up on the hill
and saw a bush on fire. When he got close, he saw that the fire was
not burning up the bush, and he realized God was there. He took
off his shoes because the ground was holy. God told Moses that
he was now God's leader and God would help him lead Israel to
the Promised Land. Moses had a lot of questions, but he obeyed
God, and God used him to free Israel from slavery in Egypt.

After hearing the story, ask questions such as the following:

- Why do you think God made sure the fire never burned
  the bush?
- Why do you think Moses took off his shoes to show the
  ground was holy?
- How can we treat the places where we find the presence
  of God?

Prayer (Together)

*You can use the words of this prayer, or see Creating Family
Prayers on page 10.*

God of the burning bush, thank you for sending Moses to
help your people. Send me to take care of the places where
you are present. Amen.

Tent of Meeting

Exodus 33:7-10

THEME: *Living in a temporary place
such as the campsite*

Claim the Time

As a signal for the beginning of devotional time, sing a simple song, such as "The Lord Is Good to Me," or one verse of "Great Is Thy Faithfulness." Or you can paraphrase a verse from a psalm, such as "We will tell the glorious deeds of the LORD and the wonders God has done" (Psalm 78:4).

A Way to Begin

Encourage group members to tell about another time they were away from home. Invite them to tell how they feel about being away from home.

Something to Do

Ask group members to walk around the outside and inside of the tent/cabin/RV and find four ways their temporary home is like their permanent home. When group members come back, record their discoveries. Have the family group members walk around outside and inside of the tent/cabin/RV and find four ways in which their temporary home is different than their permanent home. Again when group members are back together, have someone write down everyone's ideas. As everyone is exploring, you can ask questions such as the following:

- What did you discover about the similarities and the differences?
- What do you like best about living in this temporary home?
- Where do you think God will be during the time we live in our temporary home?

Bible Discovery

Introduce today's story from the Old Testament. Explain that it is about the tent in the wilderness where God met Israel. Tell, read, or act out this story. Older children can read Exodus 33:7-10 from a contemporary version of the Bible.

The Israelites were living in temporary homes as they traveled across the desert. They had been slaves in Egypt and were now on their way to the new land God had promised to give them. Their homes were tents that they had to move each day as they traveled. The Israelites believed that God was present with them during their desert journey. God's presence appeared to them in a pillar of clouds they saw during the daytime and as a pillar of fire they saw at night. Whenever the people of Israel made camp at night, they put up a "tent of meeting" that was a place for God away from the rest of the tents. When Moses went into the tent of meeting, the pillar of clouds would stand at the entrance of the tent. There Moses would speak face-to-face with God.

After you hear the story, ask questions such as the following:

- Why do you think God went with the Israelites on their journey?
- Why do you think they made a tent of meeting for God?
- How can we remember that God is with us in our temporary home?

Prayer (Together)

You can use the words of this prayer, or see Creating Family Prayers on page 10.

God of clouds and fire, be with us as we live in our temporary home. Be with me as I eat and talk and hike and explore and have fun. Amen.

Food in the Wilderness

Exodus 16:1-6

THEME: *God's good gift of food*

Claim the Time

As a signal for the beginning of devotional time, sing a simple song, such as "The Lord Is Good to Me," or one verse of "Great Is Thy Faithfulness." Or you can paraphrase a verse from a psalm, such as "We will tell the glorious deeds of the LORD and the wonders God has done" (Psalm 78:4).

A Way to Begin

Encourage group members to tell which camp food they like best and what food from back home they miss the most. Ask if they ever want to complain and go back home right away.

Something to Do

Tell group members that today they are going on a picnic to enjoy some foods like the people in Bible times ate. Pack up the food you brought (see the suggested list on page 47), a blanket, and some water to drink. Decide together where you want to go for the picnic. Explain that the foods are very simple and are either natural or have few ingredients. Remind everyone that in Bible times there were no grocery stores or factories that added ingredients to food to give them color or flavor or make them last a long time. As everyone is eating, you can ask questions such as the following:

- What do you like about these foods?
- What do you think of the idea of just eating foods that are natural or have no factory ingredients?
- What kinds of food—natural or manufactured—are most beneficial to creation?

Bible Discovery

Introduce today's story from the Old Testament. Explain that it tells about the food God gave Israel in the wilderness. Tell, read, or act out this story. Older children can read Exodus 16:1-6 from a contemporary version of the Bible.

Moses led the people of Israel out of slavery in Egypt, across the Red Sea, and into the desert. God renewed the promise that God made to Abraham and to Jacob to give them a new and wonderful land. God led them across the desert toward this new land. But all of Jacob's ancestors complained some more to God even out in the desert: "We want to go back to Egypt. There is no food here for us and no houses." God heard their complaints and sent them manna in the morning and quail at night to feed them. Manna was a kind of flaky bread that settled on the land with the dew. The people could only collect enough for one day and had to believe that God would give them more manna again the next day.

After you have heard the story, ask the following questions:

- How do you think God felt when all of Jacob's ancestors complained?
- Why do you think God gave them only enough food for one day?
- What kind of Bible food that you ate on the picnic would you like to eat again after you go home?

Prayer (Together)

You can use the words of this prayer, or see Creating Family Prayers on page 10.

God, thank you for taking care of Jacob's family when they were in the wilderness. Take care of me when I am away from home too. Amen.

Bible Times Food for Week 2:
Food in the Wilderness

A variety of foods come from the Middle East. People probably ate them in Bible times, and they are still eaten today. Choose a few from the following list for your Old Testament picnic. Since this is your lunch, be sure you also have something that everyone will eat.

Olives
Hummus—a spread made from chick peas
Cucumbers
Pita bread
Grapes
Lentils
Raisins
Figs
Dates
Chicken or lamb

Resting and Remembering

Exodus 20:8-11

THEME: *The importance of rest and memories*

Claim the Time

As a signal for the beginning of devotional time, sing a simple song, such as "The Lord Is Good to Me," or one verse of "Great Is Thy Faithfulness." Or you can paraphrase a verse from a psalm, such as "We will tell the glorious deeds of the LORD and the wonders God has done" (Psalm 78:4).

A Way to Begin

Invite group members to share some memories they have about camping so far. Remind them that some of the memories may be about God. Encourage them to share memories of what God has done on the camping trip. Ask when they have had a time to rest during the camping trip.

Something to Do

Go to a place at the campsite where group members like to go. Encourage them to lie down and look around at the sky and nature. Remind them that things in nature rest, such as animals hibernating and trees losing their leaves in the fall. As you are resting, you can ask questions such as the following:

- What are some examples of the ways that animals and plants rest?
- Why do you think it is part of God's plan for nature to rest?
- What do you like best about resting?
- What is one memory of time at camp you will take home with you?

Bible Discovery

Introduce today's story from the Old Testament. Explain that it tells about one of the commandments God gave to Israel. Tell, read, or act out this story. Older children can read the story in Exodus 20:8-11 from a contemporary version of the Bible.

When the people of Israel were on their way to the Promised Land, God spoke to Moses and told him to go to the top of a mountain. On the top of the mountain, God gave Moses tablets of stone. Written on the stones were the rules God wanted Israel to follow, called the Ten Commandments. One said that God's people were to remember that God created the whole world in six days and on the seventh day God rested. God wanted Israel to rest and to remember. God wanted them to stop their work and rest for one day—the Sabbath. On that day they were to remember all the things that God had done.

After you have heard the story, ask the following questions:

- Why do you think God wanted Israel to spend one whole day resting and remembering what God had done?
- Do you think it is a good idea to spend time resting and remembering?
- What are some ways we can rest and remember here at the campsite and after we go home?

Prayer (Together)

You can use the words of this prayer, or see Creating Family Prayers on page 10.

God of the Sabbath, thank you for giving us rules to help us be your people. Help me to spend time each day resting and remembering what you have done. Amen.

God Gives the Good Land

Deuteronomy 8:7-10

THEME: *God's good gifts*

Claim the Time

As a signal for the beginning of devotional time, sing a simple song, such as "The Lord Is Good to Me," or one verse of "Great Is Thy Faithfulness." Or you can paraphrase a verse from a psalm, such as "We will tell the glorious deeds of the LORD and the wonders God has done" (Psalm 78:4).

A Way to Begin

Remind group members that creation is full of God's wonderful gifts. Invite them to tell which gifts from God they like best.

Something to Do

Tell group members they are going to have a chance to walk around the campsite and look for one gift from God they like best. Tell them to look for an animal or a plant or a beautiful sight. Remind everyone to stay in sight of the other members of the family group. After five minutes, walk together to the gift each person has chosen so they can share why they chose that thing as the good gift from God. At each gift, ask the family group to name something they can do to take care of this gift so it will be there for others to see. As you are walking, you can ask questions such as the following:

- Why do you think God gave us these wonderful gifts?
- Why is it important to take care of God's good gifts?
- How can you thank God for these good gifts?

Bible Discovery

Introduce today's story from the Old Testament. Explain that it tells about the new land God gave to Israel. Tell, read, or act out this story. Older children can read Deuteronomy 8:7-10 from a contemporary version of the Bible.

For forty years the Israelites traveled toward the land God promised to them. It took them a long time because they forgot again and again about God and worshiped other gods. But God continued to love them, and eventually they got to the land God promised them. God told them what this new land was like and how wonderful it was. "The land has streams of water, valleys and hills; it has fertile soil where wheat and barley grow; there are lots of fruit trees with figs and pomegranates; there are lots of honey and olives. There is no shortage of good things." God wanted God's people to have all these wonderful things. God told them that they would eat and never be hungry. In turn, the people would thank God for the many blessings of the land.

After hearing the story, ask questions such as the following:

- What do you think was the most wonderful part of this new land?
- Why did God give Israel all these good things? What did God want them to do to care for the gifts?
- What part of this story do you want to remember when you go home?

Prayer (Together)

You can use the words of this prayer, or see Creating Family Prayers on page 10.

Thank you, thank you, thank you, God, for all your good gifts. Help me to take good care of them. Amen.

Songs and Prayers of Israel

Poetry from the Psalms

Introduction

Whenever we go to church today, we engage in a number of familiar songs and prayers—such as the Lord's Prayer, the *Doxology*, and the Apostles' Creed—that are a part of our community worship tradition. In the same way, the ancient Israelites used the psalms as a part of personal and corporate worship. The book of psalms is the collection of songs and prayers of our faith ancestors.

Once upon a time, church folk believed that all the Psalms came from the hand of King David. As modern biblical scholarship has evolved, scholars have learned more about the ancient language of the Hebrews. Using this knowledge, they have been able to date the Psalms and assign them to different eras within Israel's history based on the style of the language. Now many scholars believe that only Psalms 3–41 and 51–72 can be traced to David's time (although it is unlikely he himself wrote them).

Though the centuries of Judaism and church history, the Psalms have been used in corporate worship and for private devotions. Believers have loved them for their familiar and comforting words, repeated them as parts of worship, and taught them to their children as part of the tradition of the faith. Within the modern church, the translation of the Psalms from the King James Bible have been memorized and passed on to others. More recent translations now help readers find new meaning in the old words.

The topic of all of the Psalms is God and some aspect of human condition and/or their relationship to God. Specific themes about God run through the collection of Psalms. God is proclaimed as both the one who creates and the one who saves. These acts of salvation and creation made God the Lord over all nations, peoples, and creatures. The Psalmists use words such as *faithful, holy, just, powerful, righteous,* and *steadfast* to describe God and God's behavior.

There are five basic types of Psalms: prayers for help for an individual, thanksgiving songs of individuals, corporate prayers for help, psalms of instruction, and hymns. A few Psalms don't fit into these categories and were used for such things as procession, thanksgiving after victories in war, and speech in legal proceedings.

This week's Psalms are hymns of praise and thanksgiving. The focus of these Psalms is on the God of creation and the wonderful things that God has made. They express the writers' responses of gratitude and awe. As you read the Psalms with your children this week, help them to find their own wonder in the works of God in creation and discover their own words and expression of praise and thanksgiving.

The translation of the Psalms quoted this week comes from the Contemporary English Version. It is a translation of the original Hebrew that uses common language for the ancient words of the Psalmists. You can read the words included here or use another translation. Help your children to listen to the rhythm of the words and imagine all the people who have loved them over all the years since their writing.

Supplies You Will Need This Week

Paper lunch bags, several plastic containers,
    and an eyedropper
Paper and pencils or pens
Ball of yarn or string
Paper plates, paper towel tubes, or plastic container
Dry beans, rice, or pebbles
Stapler and tape

Praise the Lord

Psalm 136:1-9

THEME: *God's creation reminds us of God's love*

Claim the Time

As a signal for the beginning of devotional time, sing a simple song, such as "His Name Is Wonderful" or "This Is the Day." Or you can say a Psalm verse, such as "Clap your hands, all you peoples; shout to God with loud shouts of joy" (Psalm 47:1).

A Way to Begin

Invite group members to name one part of creation that reminds them of God's love for them. Ask them to share why this reminds them of God's love.

Something to Do

Tell family members you are going a scavenger hunt. Explain that instead of an individual hunt, the whole family group is going to walk around together and look for certain items in creation. See how many things you can find together. Notice on the list that you will be collecting different numbers of each thing. When the walk is over, you can ask questions such as the following:

- What did you most like finding? What was the hardest thing to find and why?
- Which things had you never noticed before?
- What are some other ways we can pay attention to things in creation here at the campsite and after we go home?

Bible Discovery

Introduce the day's Psalm. Explain that this Psalm is a song of praise. Try reading it responsively. Have one person or group read the first part of each line, and all other group members can respond together, saying, "God's love never fails." Place all the things you found on the scavenger hunt in the center of the group and stand where you can see the sky as you read the Psalm.

Praise the LORD! He is good.
God's love never fails.
Praise the God of all gods.
God's love never fails.
Praise the Lord of lords.
God's love never fails.
Only God works great miracles.
God's love never fails.
With wisdom he made the sky.
God's love never fails.
The Lord stretched the earth over the ocean.
God's love never fails.
He made the bright lights in the sky.
God's love never fails.
He lets the sun rule each day.
God's love never fails.
He lets the moon and the stars rule each night.
God's love never fails.

After you read the Psalm, ask the following questions:

• What did you like about the way we read the Psalm?
• What do you like best about the sky?
• What are some ways we can praise God here at the campsite and after we go home?

Prayer (Together)

You can use the words of this prayer, or see Creating Family Prayers on page 10.

God of great and wonderful love, thank you for showing us your love through your creation. Help us to pay attention to all the things in creation that remind us of your love. Amen.

Scavenger Hunt List for Week 3: Praise the Lord

You will need to take the following things to collect items on the scavenger hike: paper bag(s), glass or plastic bottle, paper and pencil, eyedropper and small container.

Here is a suggested list of things you can look for on your scavenger hike. Make changes to the list according to the ecosystem near your campsite.

1 bird feather
2 sounds from nature (make a list)
3 insects (collect in a plastic container and release them at the end of the walk)
4 different kinds of wildflowers (be sure to leave at least six of each kind still growing—and be sure not to pick any protected varieties!)
5 nuts (such as acorns or pinecones)
6 pieces of trash
7 downed twigs
8 pieces of grass
9 rocks or pebbles
10 leaves off the ground from as many different trees as possible
11 drops of water (measure with eye dropper and place in container)
12 seed pods (off grasses, trees, or flowers)

Sing a New Song
Psalm 98:1a, 4-9
THEME: *Being happy*

Claim the Time

As a signal for the beginning of devotional time, sing a simple song, such as "His Name Is Wonderful" or "This Is the Day." Or you can say a Psalm verse, such as "Clap your hands, all you peoples; shout to God with loud shouts of joy" (Psalm 47:1).

A Way to Begin

Invite group members to name a time when they were very happy. Ask them to tell what made them happy and what they did to show their happiness.

Something to Do

Remind group members that one of the ways people show their happiness is to sing happy songs and play musical instruments. Explain that they can make a song to God about how happy they are about the wonders of creation and make musical instruments from nature. Go to a place where the family group likes to go. Encourage them to think of things in nature that make them feel happy, and invite them to make a song using a tune they know. Follow the directions to make the musical shakers. As you are looking around, you can ask questions such as the following:

- What in creation makes you feel really happy?
- What is a song we can sing to tell God how happy we are?
- What kind of songs do you think the trees and birds and water sing to God?

Bible Discovery

Introduce the Psalm for the day. Explain that it describes how happy the writer is about God's goodness in making all of creation. Read the Psalm out loud together. Sing a song of praise that you like or the one you wrote. Keep time by shaking the musical shakers.

> Sing a new song to the LORD! . . .
> Tell everyone on this earth
>   to sing happy songs in praise of the LORD.
> Make music for him on harps. Play beautiful melodies!
> Sound the trumpets and horns
> and celebrate with joyful songs for our LORD and King!
> Command the ocean to roar with all of its creatures,
>   and the earth to shout with all of its people.
> Order the rivers to clap their hands,
>   and all of the hills to sing together.
> Let them worship the LORD!

After you read the Psalm, you can ask the following questions:

- Why do you think God likes happy songs?
- What do you like best about singing happy songs?
- What are other times we can use our musical shakers here at the campsite and after we go home?

Prayer (Together)

You can use the words of this prayer, or see Creating Family Prayers on page 10.

> Dear God, thank you for all of the wonderful things you have made. Help me to always remember to be happy when I look at your creation. Amen.

Make Musical Shakers for Week 3: "Sing a New Song"

There are several ways to make musical shakers to accompany your singing today. You can use the following:

- Paper plates
- Clean plastic container or bottle with a lid
- Empty paper towel or toilet paper tube

Use markers or crayons to decorate the plates, bottles, or tubes. After everyone has finished decorating the plates, containers, or tubes, pass around dry beans, rice, or small pebbles. Help the children put the beans, rice, or pebbles

1. between the paper plates and staple them together,
2. inside the plastic container and seal the lid with tape, or
3. inside the tube and cover both ends by attaching paper with tape.

Once the beans, rice, or pebbles are contained, everyone can shake the containers in time to singing.

God Cares for Creatures

Psalm 104:10-18, 21-22, 24

THEME: *Connections*

Claim the Time

As a signal for the beginning of devotional time, sing a simple song, such as "His Name Is Wonderful" or "This Is the Day." Or you can say a Psalm verse, such as "Clap your hands, all you peoples; shout to God with loud shouts of joy" (Psalm 47:1).

A Way to Begin

Invite group members to think about ways that things are connected in families and in creation. Have them name people with whom they are connected. Encourage them to name things in creation that are connected.

Something to Do

Stand in a circle and throw yarn back and forth to make a web. Have one person try to leave or sit down or turn around without dropping the yarn. Talk about what happens to the other members of the family group when they do that. Take a walk to identify connections in nature. Talk about what would happen to the squirrels if there were no acorns, or birds if there were no worms, or fish if there were no fresh water. As you are walking around, you can ask questions such as the following:

- What are some parts of nature that are connected to others?
- Why do you think God made everything connected?
- What happens if one part is damaged?

Bible Discovery

Introduce the Psalm for the day. Explain that it describes the food and homes that God has made for all the creatures. Read the Psalm out loud together. Stand under trees or by water as you read the Psalm.

> You provide streams of water in the hills and valleys,
> so that the donkeys and other wild animals can satisfy
> their thirst.
> Birds build their nests nearby and sing in the trees.
> From your home above you send rain on the hills and
> water the earth.
> You let the earth produce grass for cattle,
> plants for our food, wine to cheer us up,
> olive oil for our skin, and grain for our health.
> Our LORD, your trees always have water,
> and so do the cedars you planted in Lebanon.
> Birds nest in those trees,
> and storks make their home in the fir trees.
> Wild goats find a home in the tall mountains,
> and small animals can hide between the rocks. . . .
> Lions roar as they hunt for the food you provide.
> But when morning comes, they return to their dens. . . .
> Our LORD, by your wisdom you made so many things;
> the whole earth is covered with your living creatures.

After you read the Psalm, ask questions such as the following:

- What are some creatures we can add verses about?
- What are some plants we can add verses about?

Prayer (Together)

You can use the words of this prayer, or see Creating Family Prayers on page 10.

> God of all creatures, thank you for making the food and the houses they need. Help me to be careful so I don't destroy any of the connections. Amen.

Who Are Humans?

Psalm 8:1, 3-9

THEME: *Partners*

Claim the Time

As a signal for the beginning of devotional time, sing a simple song, such as "His Name Is Wonderful" or "This Is the Day." Or you can say a Psalm verse, such as "Clap your hands, all you peoples; shout to God with loud shouts of joy" (Psalm 47:1).

A Way to Begin

Invite group members to say how they think partners work together. Ask them to tell some ways they have been partners during the time at the campsite.

Something to Do

Explain that we were created to be partners with God. Remind group members that partners help each other and work together. Encourage them to suggest some ways they can be partners with God. Go on a walk around the campsite and look for specific things everyone can do to help God take care of creation, such as recycling, staying on paths, saving water, and so on. If you have time, ask the camp director if there is a project your family group can do to care for creation at the campsite. As you are walking around, you can ask questions such as the following:

- Who are some of the people you are a partner with?
- What is the hardest thing about being a partner?
- What is a way you can be a partner with God in caring for creation?

Bible Discovery

Introduce the Psalm for the day. Explain that it tells us God has called us to be partners to care for creation. Read the Psalm out loud together. If possible, stand outside under the stars as you read the Psalm.

> Our LORD and Ruler,
>   your name is wonderful everywhere on earth!
> You let your glory be seen in the heavens above. . . .
> I often think of the heavens your hands have made,
>   and of the moon and stars you put in place.
> Then I ask, "Why do you care about us humans?
>   Why are you concerned for us weaklings?"
> You made us a little lower than you yourself,
>   and you have crowned us with glory and honor.
> You let us rule everything your hands have made.
> And you put all of it under our power—
>   the sheep and the cattle, and every wild animal,
>   the birds in the sky, the fish in the sea,
>   and all ocean creatures.
> Our LORD and Ruler,
>   your name is wonderful everywhere on earth!

After you read the Psalm, ask questions such as the following:

- Why do you think God wants us to be partners?
- What is the most wonderful part of being God's partner?
- What are some ways to be a partner with God after we go home?

Prayer (Together)

You can use the words of this prayer, or see Creating Family Prayers on page 10.

> God of the stars and moon, thank you for asking us to be partners with you. Help me to be a good partner and do my part to care for your creation. Amen.

Sheep and Shepherds

Psalm 23

THEME: *Caring for God's creatures*

Claim the Time

As a signal for the beginning of devotional time, sing a simple song, such as "His Name Is Wonderful" or "This Is the Day." Or you can say a Psalm verse, such as "Clap your hands, all you peoples; shout to God with loud shouts of joy" (Psalm 47:1).

A Way to Begin

Invite group members to name an animal they have helped care for. Ask them specific things they did to care for the animal, such as feed and walk the dog or feed the fish, and so on. If they have never cared for an animal, invite them to tell what things need to be done.

Something to Do

Encourage group members to say what they liked about being able to care for an animal. Tell them that in Bible times there were lots of sheep and that the people who took care of them were called shepherds. The shepherds led the sheep to green grass and water; they protected them from wild animals; they called each sheep by name. The sheep knew the voice of the shepherd. Take a walk and pretend to be sheep. Take turns being the shepherd. After your walk, you can ask questions such as the following:

- Which did you like best—being a sheep or the shepherd? Why?
- What did the shepherd do to care for the sheep?
- Why do you think the sheep trusted the shepherd?

Bible Discovery

Introduce the Psalm for the day. Explain that it compares the way God takes care of people to the way the shepherd takes care of sheep. Read the Psalm out loud together. Imagine what it is like to be sheep.

> You, LORD, are my shepherd. I will never be in need.
>> You let me rest in fields of green grass.
> You lead me to streams of peaceful water,
>> and you refresh my life.
> You are true to your name,
>> and you lead me along the right paths.
> I may walk through valleys as dark as death,
>> but I won't be afraid.
> You are with me,
>> and your shepherd's rod makes me feel safe.
> You treat me to a feast, while my enemies watch.
> You honor me as your guest,
>> and you fill my cup until it overflows.
> Your kindness and love will always be with me
> each day of my life,
>> and I will live forever in your house, LORD.

After you read the Psalm, ask questions such as the following:

• Who are some people in the world today who take care of God's creatures?

• Imagine you are like a sheep. How does God take care of you?

• What are some ways we can be shepherds after we go home?

Prayer (Together)

You can use the words of this prayer, or see Creating Family Prayers on page 10.

> Shepherd God, thank you for taking care of me and meeting all my needs. Help me to trust and depend on your care. Amen.

I Am Like a Green Tree

Psalm 52:8-9

THEME: *Things that are alike*

Claim the Time

As a signal for the beginning of devotional time, sing a simple song, such as "His Name Is Wonderful" or "This Is the Day." Or you can say a Psalm verse, such as "Clap your hands, all you peoples; shout to God with loud shouts of joy" (Psalm 47:1).

A Way to Begin

Invite everyone to finish one or more of these sentences: "Rainbows are like . . ."; Waterfalls are like . . ."; "Autumn leaves are like . . ." Ask if anyone wants to make up his or her own comparison statement.

Something to Do

Go to a place near the campsite where you can see green trees. Explain that the people who wrote the Psalms liked to use comparisons. They would say, "God is like . . ." Or "I am like . . ." Encourage group members to look around at the trees and say one thing about how God is like a green tree and how they are like a green tree. Invite them to look at other parts of creation and say how God is like that part of creation or how they are like that part of creation. As you are walking around and looking at creation, you can ask questions such as the following:

- How did you like making comparisons?
- How did it help you think about God?
- What do you think was most fun?

Bible Discovery

Introduce the Psalm for the day. Explain that it describes how the writer of the Psalm is like a green tree. Read the Psalm out loud together. Stand under some trees as you read the Psalm.

I am like an olive tree growing in God's house,
   and I can count on his love forever and ever.
I will always thank God for what he has done;
   I will praise his good name when his people meet.

After you read the Psalm, ask questions such as the following:

- What do you think it would be like to be a tree?
- When do you count on God's love?
- What is a way we can show our trust in God's goodness here at the campsite and after we go home?

Prayer (Together)

You can use the words of this prayer, or see Creating Family Prayers on page 10.

God of green trees, thank you for their deep roots and tall branches. Help me to be like a green tree and to trust your love. Amen.

The Lord Has Made This Day

Psalm 118:1, 24, 27-29

THEME: *Celebrations*

Claim the Time

As a signal for the beginning of devotional time, sing a simple song, such as "His Name Is Wonderful" or "This Is the Day." Or you can say a Psalm verse, such as "Clap your hands, all you peoples; shout to God with loud shouts of joy" (Psalm 47:1).

A Way to Begin

Invite group members to tell about a time when they were part of a celebration. Ask them to share what they were celebrating and what they did to celebrate. Encourage everyone to tell why we have celebrations.

Something to Do

Go to a place near the campsite that everyone in the family group likes. Have the group members look around and name one thing that God has made that they want to celebrate. Explain that in Bible times people waved branches and marched around to celebrate what God had done. Have group members find a branch they want to wave. Remind them to only pick up branches off the ground and not to pick a live tree. Make a parade, and walk around waving branches and praising God. After your celebration, you can ask questions such as the following:

- How did you like acknowledging what God has done by having a celebration?
- What are some other ways we can celebrate God's creation here at the campsite and after we go home?

Bible Discovery

Introduce the Psalm for the day. Explain that it is a celebration of God's goodness. Read the Psalm out loud together. Wave your branches as you read the Psalm.

> Tell the LORD how thankful you are,
>> because he is kind and always merciful.
>
> This day belongs to the LORD!
>> Let's celebrate and be glad today.
>
> The LORD is our God, and he has given us light!
> Start the celebration!
>> March with palm branches all the way to the altar.
>
> The LORD is my God!
>> I will praise him and tell him how thankful I am.
>
> Tell the LORD how thankful you are,
>> because he is kind and always merciful.

After you read the Psalm, ask questions such as the following:

- What is the best thing God has done for you today?
- How do you want to celebrate that?
- How can we celebrate God's goodness here at the campsite and after we go home?

Prayer (Together)

You can use the words of this prayer, or see Creating Family Prayers on page 10.

God of celebrations, thank you for songs and music and dance. Help me to celebrate your love every day. Amen.

Following Jesus
Stories from the Four Gospels

Introduction

Imagine what it must have been like to be a Christian in the days soon after Jesus died and rose from the grave. The men and women who had traveled with Jesus must have loved to tell stories about what Jesus did and said.

You could sit in the courtyard of someone's house in Jerusalem and listen to Peter or James or John or one of the other disciples talk about Jesus. You could ask them questions about Jesus and hear their responses. Hearing what those who had actually walked and talked with Jesus had to say must have been wonderful. It must have made Jesus seem very real and alive.

However, as the years went by and the church grew, it became more and more difficult to hear stories from the firsthand witnesses of Jesus' life. The church was spread beyond Jerusalem, and these witnesses couldn't be everywhere to tell the stories firsthand. Telling the stories became the job of the second and thirdhand witnesses.

As others took up telling the stories, some of them began to write them down. There still weren't any books about Jesus; the only Bible was the Hebrew Scriptures, what we call the Old Testament. It wasn't until forty to sixty years after Jesus died that the stories about him were written down and circulated to believers.

Four of these collections of stories form the Gospels that we have today. Four different collections of the stories were gathered by different people. Those Gospel writers decided on an order for the stories, which stories to include, and how to arrange them for a particular group of believers at a particular place.

As you tell these stories to the children this week, keep in mind the oral tradition of the early church. Help the kids to understand how people who loved Jesus told the stories before they were written down.

We have very few accounts in the Gospels of times that Jesus went inside to teach. Rather, he was outside, sitting on a rock beside the lake or rowing in a boat or walking along a dirt road. He was always on the move, and the crowd followed him almost everywhere he went.

Take the children outside to hear these stories about Jesus. Sit in the grass, stand beside the water, walk among the trees, or wander among the flowers. Help your children to imagine a Jesus who loved to be outside and who loved the creation and all its creatures.

To make the stories come alive for your children, read a story ahead of time from the devotional or the Bible. Then tell it to the children. Imagine that you were there in person when Jesus acted and spoke. Imagine the story as if you had been there. Make the story come alive for the children by telling them what you saw and heard. Invite them to imagine being there too.

Supplies You Will Need for the Week

Construction paper
Markers
Field guide for wildflowers
Paper towel
Toy boats, or 8½" x 11" white paper to fold into boats
Large pan or bowl if there is no natural body of water
    at campsite
Blindfolds
Bibles

Saying Thanks

Luke 17:11-18

THEME: *Presents*

Claim the Time

As a signal for the beginning of devotional time, sing a simple song, such as "Jesus Loves Me," or a verse from "Blessed Assurance." Or you can say, "Blessed is the one who comes in the name of the LORD" (Psalm 118:26).

A Way to Begin

Invite group members to tell about the best present they ever received. Encourage them to say what made it such a great present.

Something to Do

Remind everyone that God gives us presents too, and that today group members are going to find their favorite present from God in nature. Tell group members to spend some time walking around near the campsite and find one present from God that they really, really like. Remind group members to stay where they can see everyone else. After five minutes, call group members back together and invite everyone to tell what present from God they found that they liked best. Record the responses. In the course of the conversation about presents, ask questions such as the following:

- What surprised you most as you looked around for a present?
- What would you like to say to God for this wonderful present?
- Why is it important to say thanks to God for the wonderful presents God gives us?

Bible Discovery

Introduce the day's story from the New Testament. Explain that it tells about a time Jesus gave a wonderful present to ten men. Tell, read, or act out this story. Older children can read Luke 17:11-18 from a contemporary version of the Bible.

One day Jesus was walking along a road and saw some people called lepers. Lepers had to live alone and far away from other people in town because they had a contagious skin disease called leprosy. The Jewish religious leaders believed that the lepers had broken some religious law, so they called the lepers "unclean" and told them they could not come to worship. When the lepers saw Jesus that day, they asked him to help them. He told them to go see the priests. Only the priests could decide if they were "clean." On the way the lepers noticed something wonderful. Their skin was healed. Jesus had healed them. Wow! Nine of the men ran to the priests and then home to their families. One of the men stopped, went back to Jesus, and thanked him. He was very glad to be healed and well again.

Ask some questions such as the following:
- Why do you think the one man came back to thank Jesus?
- What would you have done if you had been one of the ten lepers?
- What are some ways we can thank God and one another for wonderful presents during camp time and after we go home?

Prayer (Together)

You can use the words of this prayer, or see Creating Family Prayers on page 10.

Thank you, God, for all the wonderful presents you gave us in creation. Help me to remember to say thank you for your presents. Amen.

A Boy and His Lunch

John 6:1-14

THEME: *Sharing food together*

Claim the Time

As a signal for the beginning of devotional time, sing a simple song, such as "Jesus Loves Me," or a verse from "Blessed Assurance." Or you can say, "Blessed is the one who comes in the name of the LORD" (Psalm 118:26).

A Way to Begin

Explain that you are going on a picnic today. Ask group members what they like best about picnics.

Something to Do

Talk together about what food to take and where to go for the picnic. Work together to make the lunch and pack it. Make a list of everything you will need, and let everyone help collect those things, such as a quilt or blanket, water bottles, sunscreen, bug spray, and so on. As you are preparing for the picnic, ask questions such as the following:

- What are some other picnics that you remember?
- What are some things that happened on other picnics?
- What part of picnics don't you enjoy?
- What is something you would like to do during the time we are having our picnic?

Bible Discovery

Introduce the day's story of the feeding of the five thousand. Explain that the story is about a time when Jesus hosted a picnic for five thousand people and the only food available was a small boy's lunch. Tell, read, or act out this story. Older children can read John 6:1-14 from a contemporary version of the Bible.

One day Jesus was teaching and healing people on a mountain near the Sea of Galilee. There were lots and lots of people. As dinnertime drew near, his disciples came to him and pointed out that no one had any food and that they were hungry. Andrew, one of the disciples, brought to Jesus a small boy who had a picnic lunch of five little loaves of bread and two fish. Today maybe he would have a tuna fish sandwich. Everyone wondered what Jesus would do. How could Jesus feed five thousand people with just one boy's lunch? Jesus took the bread and fish and gave thanks to God for them. Then his disciples passed out the food to everyone. Guess what! Everybody had enough to eat and there was even food left over.

Ask questions such as the following:

- Why do you think Jesus said thank you to God before he passed out the food?
- Why is it important for us to say thanks to God before we eat?
- How would you feel if Jesus asked you to share your lunch?

Prayer (Together)

You can use the words of this prayer, or see Creating Family Prayers on page 10.

Thank you, God, for our picnic lunch—for (name the foods in your picnic). Thank you for fun on our picnic and for everyone eating together. Help me to remember people who are hungry. Amen.

Lilies and Birds

Matthew 6:25-32

THEME: *God's wonderful care for all creation*

Claim the Time

As a signal for the beginning of devotional time, sing a simple song, such as "Jesus Loves Me," or a verse from "Blessed Assurance." Or you can say, "Blessed is the one who comes in the name of the LORD" (Psalm 118:26).

A Way to Begin

Explain to group members that today they are going to have a chance to look at the wildflowers around camp. Ask everyone to say one thing they like about flowers.

Something to Do

Tell group members to find one wildflower that they really like. Don't pick it! Just encourage everyone to notice the color of the flower and how it grows. Remind group members to stay where they can see everyone else. After five minutes, call group members back together. As a group, walk around to each flower and have the person who chose it say what he or she liked best about the flower. If you have a field guide for flowers in the area, you can identify them and find out additional information. As you are looking at the different flowers, you can ask questions such as the following:

- What do you like best about the flower you found?
- What is one thing God does to care for the flowers?
- What is one thing we can do to care for the flowers?

Bible Discovery

Introduce the day's story from the New Testament. Explain that it tells about a time when Jesus taught the people about God. Tell, read, or act out this story. Older children can read the story from Matthew 6:25-32 from a contemporary version of the Bible.

One day Jesus was sitting on a mountainside teaching a crowd of people about God. He wanted them to know that God loved them and would take care of them. He didn't want them to worry about their food or drink or clothing. Jesus told the people to look around and to notice the birds of the air and the lilies of the field. God takes care of them and gives them food and water and sun and homes. They are all beautiful—even the marvelous temple that King Solomon built is not as beautiful as they are. "Please don't worry," Jesus said. "Trust God. God will care for you even better than he does the flowers."

After sharing the Bible story, ask the following questions:

- How does God take care of us?
- What do you worry about?
- What do you think Jesus would say to you about your worries if he was here right now?

Prayer (Together)

You can use the words of this prayer, or see Creating Family Prayers on page 10.

Thank you, God, for the beautiful flowers and birds you have made. Thank you for taking care of them and for taking care of me. Help me not to worry. Amen.

Directions for Preserving Flowers for Week 4: "Lilies and Birds"

You can save some flowers and take them home with you if you would like. Keep in mind, however, that conservationists tell us that it is important to leave six wildflowers for every one we pick. And be sure to avoid picking any protected varieties, which would not only be poor creation care but also risk incurring a fine!

Pick one flower of each kind you found and layer each one between two pieces of paper towel. Put something heavy on the flowers in the towel. In a few days you will notice that the flowers are beginning to dry out.

When you get home, you can press the flowers further until they are completely dry. Then place the flowers between sheets of clear contact paper. You will have them to remember your camping trip. Mark them with the date you found them and the location. Record the information you found in the field guide about each flower.

Jesus Blesses the Children

Matthew 19:13-15

THEME: *God's care and love for small things.*

Claim the Time

As a signal for the beginning of devotional time, sing a simple song, such as "Jesus Loves Me," or a verse from "Blessed Assurance." Or you can say, "Blessed is the one who comes in the name of the LORD" (Psalm 118:26).

A Way to Begin

Explain to group members that today everyone is going to look for small things in creation and hear a story about Jesus and children. Ask group members why they think children and other small things are important.

Something to Do

Have group members look around and find three small things. Have them come back to tell everyone what they have found. Explain that if what they find is not living and can be carried, they can bring it back to show to everyone. Give everyone five minutes to search for small things in creation. Gather everyone back together, and invite each person to tell what small things he or she found. Have group members show and tell and talk about the role each thing they found has in creation; for example, seeds make new plants, ants clean up, bees make honey. During the sharing time, ask questions such as the following:

- Why are small things important and valuable?
- What would happen in nature if these small things you found didn't exist?
- What is the best thing about being small?

Bible Discovery

Introduce the day's story about Jesus. Explain that the story is about a time when Jesus talked to the children and blessed them. Tell, read, or act out this story. Older children can read Matthew 19:13-15 from a contemporary version of the Bible.

Jesus liked children. He liked to talk to them and to hear what they had to say. He invited them to be close to him so he could bless them. Mothers and fathers liked to bring their children to see Jesus. Some grownups didn't think Jesus should waste his time with children. Even his disciples told the parents not to bother Jesus. In those days many grown-ups didn't think children were very important or valuable. They thought that children were only worthwhile when they grew up and could earn money or get married. Jesus said that children were important and valuable to God right now and were part of God's kingdom and family.

As you are talking about this story, ask questions such as the following:

- How do you think the children felt when Jesus blessed them?
- How would you feel if Jesus were here right now? What would you like to ask him?
- What things can we do while camping and after we go back home to remember God's love for children and small things?

Prayer (Together)

You can use the words of this prayer, or see Creating Family Prayers on page 10.

Thank you, Jesus, for loving the little children and blessing them. Thank you for loving me and blessing me. Amen.

Storm on the Lake

Mark 4:35-41

THEME: *Boats and storms*

Claim the Time

As a signal for the beginning of devotional time, sing a simple song, such as "Jesus Loves Me," or a verse from "Blessed Assurance." Or you can say, "Blessed is the one who comes in the name of the LORD" (Psalm 118:26).

A Way to Begin

Invite group members to talk about times they have been out in boats. Encourage them to talk about how they would feel if a storm came up when they were out in a boat.

Something to Do

Walk to a body of water near where you are camping, or fill a large bowl or tub with water. Take along several small toy boats or a piece of plain white paper for everyone. When you are settled beside the water, put the plastic or wooden boats in the water or follow the instructions on pages 84–87 to make paper boats. Have everyone watch the boats floating on the water. Take turns stirring up the water to make it move. Put your hand on the water and make the water be still. As everyone watches the boats, ask questions such as the following:

- What do the boats do when the water isn't moving?
- What happens to the boats when we stir up the water?
- How do you think people in the boats would feel when the boat was tossed about by the waves?

Bible Discovery

Introduce the day's story. Explain that it is about a time when Jesus and his disciples were out in a boat on a large lake. Tell, read, or act out this story. Older children can read Mark 4:35-41 from a contemporary version of the Bible.

In the country where Jesus lived, there was a big lake called the Sea of Galilee. Sometimes big storms came up suddenly on the lake. One day Jesus said, "It's been a long day. Let's take a boat out on the lake." The disciples rowed the boat, and Jesus went to sleep. Suddenly there was a big storm. The wind blew, waves crashed over the side of the boat, and rain poured down. The disciples were frightened, but Jesus kept on sleeping. The men yelled to wake him up. When Jesus woke up, he stood in the front of the boat and spoke to the wind and waves and rain. He told them to stop. And the wind and waves and rain stopped. The disciples were amazed and Jesus said to them, "Why didn't you trust me to take care of you—even in the storm?"

After hearing the story, ask questions such as the following:

- How do you think the men felt when Jesus made the storm stop?
- What does it mean to trust Jesus to take care of you?
- What are some ways we can show our trust in Jesus' care during camping and after we go home?

Prayer (Together)

You can use the words of this prayer, or see Creating Family Prayers on page 10.

Thank you, God for our time playing with the boats. Help me to trust you to take care of me and my family and all your people and creatures. Amen.

For Week 4, "Storm on the Lake"
Directions for Folding Paper Boats

1. Take an 8½ x 11-inch sheet of copy and print paper. Fold the upper half down on the dotted (center) line.

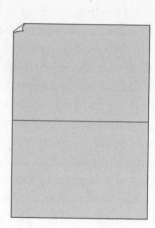

2. Find the center line by folding the left side to the right side and then unfolding.

3. Fold downward both upper triangles on the dotted lines.

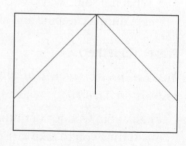

4. It must look like this.

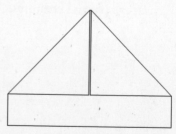

5. At the bottom, fold the top layer upward to align with the bottom of the triangles.

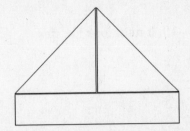

6. Fold the two small triangles on the left and on the right backward to make them disappear.

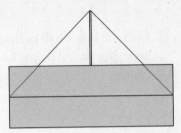

7. It must look like this.

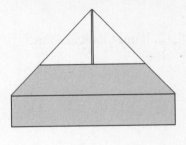

8. Turn the paper over and fold the other lower strip upward. You have formed the well-known hat.

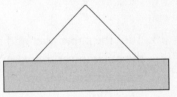

9. Turn the hat 90 degrees and open it. The thumbs must be inside. Flatten the upper and the lower parts on each other to form a square diamond.

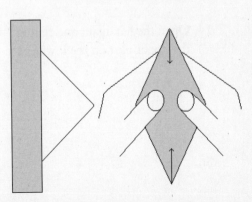

10. It must look like this.

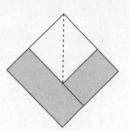

11. Fold the lower half of the front triangle upward on the horizontal center.

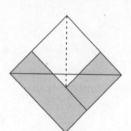

12. It must look like this.

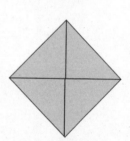

13. Turn the paper over and fold up the other lower triangle. You get a hat without a brim.

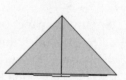

14. Open the hat again and flatten the upper part on the lower part.

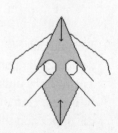

15. Pull the upper corners of the triangles in direction of the arrows.

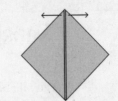

16. If using 8½ x 11-inch copy and print paper, the sail will be visible above the sides of the boat.

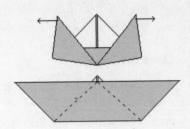

17. Stretch the boat both to the right and left, and then separate it slightly from underneath so it can float.

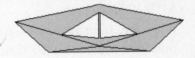

Seaside Cookout

John 21:1-12

THEME: *Sharing a meal together*

Claim the Time

As a signal for the beginning of devotional time, sing a simple song, such as "Jesus Loves Me," or a verse from "Blessed Assurance." Or you can say, "Blessed is the one who comes in the name of the LORD" (Psalm 118:26).

A Way to Begin

Invite group members to name a time they have shared in the preparation of a meal. Ask them what they needed to do and what food they served.

Something to Do

Make plans to cook breakfast over a campfire or a camp stove. (If this is not possible, take your prepared breakfast outside to eat.) Decide ahead of time what you will eat and how you will cook it. Involve everyone in helping by making a list of what needs to be done and who is going to do it. As the breakfast cooks, encourage everyone to think about the colors of the food and the smells as it is cooking. As you eat the breakfast, invite group members to think about what they like about cooking and eating together. As you are eating, ask questions such as the following:

- What smells did you notice as the breakfast cooked? What colors did you see?
- What did you enjoy most about cooking and eating breakfast together outside?
- Imagine that Jesus has come to our cookout breakfast. What do you think he would say or do?

Bible Discovery

Introduce the story about a time when Jesus had a breakfast cook-out with his disciples. Explain that the story takes place after the resurrection. Tell, read, or act out this story. Older children can read John 21:1-12 from a contemporary version of the Bible.

After Jesus died, he appeared to his disciples several times to show them he was alive and to explain that he was going away. The disciples were sad that Jesus was leaving. The ones who had been fishermen before they decided to follow Jesus went fishing. One morning after they had been fishing all night, they noticed a figure on the shore of the lake. The man called out to ask them how many fish they had caught, and they replied that they had caught nothing all night long. The man told them to put the nets out on the other side of the boat. Suddenly the nets were full of fish! Peter was the first to recognize Jesus, and he jumped over-board and swam back to shore while the others rowed the boat. Jesus had a fire going and told them to bring the fish to cook. "Let's have breakfast together," he said. So that is exactly what they did.

After hearing the story, ask questions such as the following:

- How do you think the disciples felt when they realized the man on shore was Jesus?
- What do you think of the idea of Jesus doing something ordinary like cooking breakfast for his friends?
- What are some other things we can share together today?

Prayer (Together)

You can use the words of this prayer, or see Creating Family Prayers on page 10.

God of good things, thank you for food to eat and for hav-ing fun together. Help me remember to welcome you at every meal and in every activity throughout the day. Amen.

The Little Man and the Tree
Luke 19:1-10
THEME: *Trees*

Claim the Time

As a signal for the beginning of devotional time, sing a simple song, such as "Jesus Loves Me," or a verse from "Blessed Assurance." Or you can say, "Blessed is the one who comes in the name of the LORD" (Psalm 118:26).

A Way to Begin

Invite group members to share something they like about trees.

Something to Do

Walk to a place where there are lots of trees. Invite group members to say one thing they notice about trees; for example, they are tall, they have leaves, they are homes for animals. Explain that group members will have a chance to get to know one tree really well. One by one each person will be blindfolded and led by the others to a tree. The "blind" person will then explore the tree by touching, smelling, and listening. When the person is led back to the group and the blindfold is removed, the person will see if he or she can find the tree. With a larger group, divide into pairs and take turns being blind. If you have a field guide for trees in the area, use it to find out what kind each tree is. Gather together afterward and ask questions such as the following:

- How did you find your tree?
- What was hard about being blind?
- What do you think you could see from the top of the tree?

Bible Discovery

Introduce the story of Zacchaeus. Explain that this story is about a small man who climbed a tree to see Jesus and what happened afterward. Tell, read, or act out this story. Older children can read Luke 19:1-10 from a contemporary version of the Bible.

Zacchaeus was a very short man, and his job was to collect taxes. Not very many people liked Zacchaeus, because sometimes he collected extra money and kept it for himself. One day Jesus came to the town where Zacchaeus lived, and Zacchaeus wanted to see Jesus. Zacchaeus had to climb a tree so he could see Jesus. Jesus stopped at the bottom of the tree and spoke to Zacchaeus. "Come down from the tree, Zacchaeus. I want to come to your house for dinner." Zacchaeus was amazed. Jesus told him he knew all about him and wanted to come to dinner all the same. After dinner Zacchaeus went around the village and gave back all the extra money he had taken from people.

After the story, ask questions such as the following:

- What was the best thing that happened in this story?
- Where do you go to see Jesus?
- What are some ways we can show we know Jesus here at the campsite and after we go home?

Prayer (Together)

You can use the words of this prayer, or see Creating Family Prayers on page 10.

God of tall trees and little people, thank you for the gift of trees. Forgive me when I make mistakes, and help me to ask forgiveness of others. Amen.

WEEK 5

Stories Jesus Told

Parables in Matthew and Luke

Introduction

Some of the most familiar stories from the New Testament are parables: the good Samaritan, the prodigal son, and the lost sheep, among many others. We may be tempted to think when we read these stories that they tell us about an actual event. However, they are stories that Jesus made up to teach something about God and about human nature.

Imagine that you have gone to hear Jesus teach. He is sitting on a large rock by the shore of the lake. People are gathered around him on the grass. Everyone is listening, and people close to him are asking him questions.

A man in the crowd asks Jesus how a person can be with God forever. Jesus has no simple answer for the very difficult question, and he asks the man what the teachings of the Old Testament say. "To love God with all your heart and mind and soul," the man replies, "and your neighbor as yourself." Jesus affirms this response and tells the man to go and do those things. The man, still hoping Jesus will give him a simple answer, asks, "Who is my neighbor?"

Jesus could have given the man a direct answer. But Jesus wanted the man to figure out the principle for himself. So Jesus told a story about a man who was attacked by robbers and left for

93

dead. People passed by and saw the victim, but only one person stopped to help. Jesus then asked, "Who acted as a neighbor in this story?"

This was not a news report about real events; it was a parable, a fictional story with a lesson tucked inside. Jesus told this parable to help his audience think about who their neighbors were. Believers from that day forward have had to reflect on the story and the difficult query Jesus threw our way. Who is your neighbor? Who is my neighbor?

Since parables are basically puzzles and because most children love figuring out puzzles, your children may really enjoy engaging with the parables. Regardless of a child's age, Jesus' questions relate to his or her life. Who is your neighbor? Well, children know about liking some kids and not liking others. The parable invites them to think about the disliked kids as their neighbors. What if it was Smelly Kelly who ran to help when he or she fell off the swing? What if Bully Ben was the one who needed their help?

Because many of Jesus' parables use illustrations from nature, they are good stories to consider while camping. They invite us to think not only of human neighbors but also of creatures and growing plants. How can we be good neighbors to them? How are they good neighbors to us? These seven parables and others can engage you and your children in conversations about different ideas regarding common, everyday stuff.

Supplies You Will Need This Week

Biscuit mix, butter or margarine, jelly (optional)
Mixing bowl and measuring cups
13 x 9-inch pan (or long sticks appropriate for use in cooking over a fire)

Parable of the Vineyard
Matthew 20:1-16
THEME: *God's generosity extends to all people*

Claim the Time

As a signal for the beginning of devotional time, sing a simple song, such as "Seek Ye First," or one verse of "Tell Me the Story of Jesus." Or you can say a Psalm verse, such as "Make me to know your ways, O LORD; teach me your paths" (Psalm 25:4).

A Way to Begin

Invite group members to share what they think are some of the wonderful gifts they have from God. Ask them how they feel about God giving them such wonderful gifts.

Something to Do

Take a walk beyond the area of the campsite—beyond any buildings or cultivated area of the campground. Look for the wonderful gifts in creation that God wants everyone to enjoy. Encourage everyone to point out such gifts—for example, a patch of wildflowers, plump berries, or wild mushrooms, a shady tree, a songbird or colorful butterfly, a clever squirrel or proud buck. As you walk along, ask questions such as the following:

- Why do you think God made such a wonderful world for us to live in?
- What people or animals are making good use of this world?
- What people or animals are abusing or neglecting God's world?

Bible Discovery

Introduce the parable of the vineyard. Explain that Jesus told this parable to help his listeners think about the extravagant and bewildering generosity of God. Tell, read, or act out this story. Older children can read Matthew 20:1-16 from a contemporary version of the Bible.

A vineyard owner hired workers to pick his grapes. Some people started at 9:00 in the morning and worked all day. The man promised them the usual daily wage. Some other people started working at noon, and the owner promised them the usual daily wage. Still other people began working at 4:00 in the afternoon and worked for only an hour. At the end of the day, the owner paid all the workers the exact same amount of money. Those who worked all day told the owner they thought that was unfair. But the owner said, "Didn't I pay you what I promised? It is my money, and I can pay my other workers whatever I want."

After hearing the parable, ask questions such as the following:

- What do you think of the owner who paid everyone the same amount regardless of how long they worked? Why?
- How is God like the owner of the vineyard?
- How can we be more generous to people here at the campsite and at home?

Prayer (Together)

You can use the words of this prayer, or see Creating Family Prayers on page 10.

Dear God, thank you for giving generous gifts to all the people in the world. Help me to be more generous with the gifts you have given to me. Amen.

Parable of the Sower

Matthew 13:1-9

THEME: *Sharing the Good News of God's kingdom*

Claim the Time

As a signal for the beginning of devotional time, sing a simple song, such as "Seek Ye First," or one verse of "Tell Me the Story of Jesus." Or you can say a Psalm verse, such as "Make me to know your ways, O LORD; teach me your paths" (Psalm 25:4).

A Way to Begin

Invite group members to share some good news they know. Ask them something they know that they want to tell everyone about.

Something to Do

Take a walk around the campsite and look at different kinds of plants. Point out the acorn that grows into an oak tree or the dandelion puff that will seed new golden flowers. Remind everyone that every plant growing around them started off as a seed. Some seeds fell straight down; others were blown in the wind; some were buried by animals and forgotten; others were eaten by birds and deposited far away. As you are walking along, ask questions such as the following:

- How much sun does the plant get? Where does the plant get water?
- What is the soil like around the plant?
- What other plants or rocks are in the way of the plant's growth?

Bible Discovery

Introduce the parable of the sower. Explain that Jesus told this parable to help his followers consider how the gospel message is like a seed. Tell, read, or act out this story. Older children can read Matthew 13:1-9 from a contemporary version of the Bible.

One day a farmer went out to plant his crop. He didn't have big machines and tractors, so he used hand tools or a donkey-pulled plow to get the soil ready. Then he threw out the seed by hand as he walked along. When he threw out a handful of seeds, some seeds fell on the path and the birds ate them; other seeds fell on rocky ground where there wasn't much soil, so they grew fast but never got deep roots; some seeds fell in a patch of weeds and the thorns choked them; but some seeds fell on good soil and grew into strong plants.

After hearing the parable, ask questions such as the following:
- How is God like the farmer planting seeds in the fields?
- How is the good news about Jesus and God's love like the seeds?
- How can we be good soil for the seeds of Jesus' love to grow here at the campsite and at home?

Prayer (Together)

You can use the words of this prayer, or see Creating Family Prayers on page 10.

God of great love, thank you for sending Jesus to tell us about your love. Help me to be good soil for your love to grow, and show me how to sow more seeds of that love in the hearts of other people. Amen.

Parable of Small Things

Luke 13:18-19

THEME: *Small beginnings*

Claim the Time

As a signal for the beginning of devotional time, sing a simple song, such as "Seek Ye First," or one verse of "Tell Me the Story of Jesus." Or you can say a Psalm verse, such as "Make me to know your ways, O LORD; teach me your paths" (Psalm 25:4).

A Way to Begin

Encourage group members to tell about a time they planted some seeds or made bread. Ask them to describe what happened to the seed and bread.

Something to Do

Gather the ingredients you need to make bread sticks. (See the recipe provided at the end of this devotion.) Allow everyone in the family group to participate in the process—measuring, adding, mixing the ingredients; kneading the dough; pressing the dough into the pan or wrapping it around sticks. Work outside if possible. And don't forget the best part: eating the bread together! As you work on the bread or later as you are eating it, ask questions such as the following:

- What are some small things that are important to you?
- What would these bread sticks be like if they didn't have some kind of leaven in them?
- What other small things have you seen grow big?

Bible Discovery

Introduce the parable of the yeast and the mustard seed. Explain that Jesus told these parables to help his listeners think about how God's kingdom—the place where God's love reigns—may start very small but grows to be very big. Tell, read, or act out this story. Older children may read Luke 13:18-19 from a contemporary version of the Bible.

One day Jesus asked those who were listening to him what they thought the kingdom of God was like. He wanted them to imagine what it would be like to live in a land ruled by God where there was always goodness, justice, and love. To help them, Jesus said that the kingdom of God is like a seed planted in a garden. It grew into such a big tree that birds could build their nests in it. The kingdom of God is like yeast that a woman took and mixed up with flour and water to make bread. The yeast made air bubbles in the flour, and the bread became twice as big.

After hearing the story, ask questions such as the following:

- What do you think of a place called the kingdom of God, where God's love rules?
- What would it be like to live in such a place?
- What are some things we can do to make our campsite more like a place where God is ruler?

Prayer (Together)

You can use the words of this prayer, or see Creating Family Prayers on page 10.

God, our loving Creator, thank you for your kingdom, where small things become something great! Help me to believe in your kingdom and live as if it is here right now. Amen.

Recipe for Bread Sticks for Week 5:
"Parable of Small Things"

1/2 cup butter or margarine
2 cups biscuit mix
1/2 cup cold water

In a medium bowl, mix together the butter/margarine, the water and biscuit mix until a soft dough forms. Place dough on a clean, hard surface dusted with biscuit mix. Roll dough on surface, shape into large ball, and knead five times. Divide into twelve equal balls and bake in one of two ways:

- Over an open fire: Wrap the ball of dough around the end of a stick and hold it over a fire until the outside of the bread is light brown and crispy. Slide the bread off the stick and enjoy while hot with butter or margarine. Or you can slide some jelly into the hole where the stick was.
- In an oven (for cabin or RV campers): Bake the bread sticks in a 13 x 9-inch pan in a 425-degree oven. Flatten each ball of dough into a rectangular bread stick. Roll in butter or margarine and place in pan. Bake for 12–15 minutes.

Parable of the Lost Sheep

Luke 15:3-7

THEME: *Lost and found*

Claim the Time

As a signal for the beginning of devotional time, sing a simple song, such as "Seek Ye First," or one verse of "Tell Me the Story of Jesus." Or you can say a Psalm verse, such as "Make me to know your ways, O LORD; teach me your paths" (Psalm 25:4).

A Way to Begin

Encourage group members to tell about a time when they lost something and then found it again later. Ask them to talk about how they felt when the object was lost and when they found it.

Something to Do

Organize a game of hide and seek by selecting a person to be It. That person should cover his or her eyes and count to twenty (or some agreed-upon number). Everyone else should hide nearby—somewhere that allows him or her to see the person who is It. When finished counting, It tries to find everyone who is hidden. Let as many people as possible be It. Play as many rounds as you want. After the game, ask questions such as the following:

- What part did you like best: finding people or hiding? Why?
- How did you feel when you were "lost"?
- How did you feel when you were "found"?
- What is the best part of finding someone else?

Bible Discovery

Introduce the parable of the lost sheep. Explain that Jesus told this parable to help his listeners understand that every creature (including every one of us) is important to God. Tell, read, or act out this story. Older children may read Luke 15:3-7 from a contemporary version of the Bible.

Once there was a shepherd who had a flock of one hundred sheep. Each one was important to the shepherd, and he knew all his sheep by name. He led them to new grass and fresh water. He protected them from dangerous animals that tried to hurt them. One day the shepherd noticed that one sheep was missing. He put the other ninety-nine sheep in a circle of piled stones and went to look for the lost one. When he found the lost sheep, he was very happy. He put the sheep on his shoulders, took it home, and told his neighbors the good news that he had found his lost sheep.

After sharing the parable, ask questions such as the following:

- Why do you think the shepherd was so glad to find the sheep?
- The shepherd's job was to take care of the sheep. What are you responsible for taking care of?
- What are some ways that we can take care of the animals that live here at the campsite? How can we care for animals (and people) when we return home?

Prayer (Together)

You can use the words of this prayer, or see Creating Family Prayers on page 10.

God of all creatures, thank you for animals of all kinds.
Help me to take good care of everything and everyone you created. Amen.

Parable of the Rich Fool
Luke 12:13-21

THEME: *Know what is really important*

Claim the Time

As a signal for the beginning of devotional time, sing a simple song, such as "Seek Ye First," or one verse of "Tell Me the Story of Jesus." Or you can say a Psalm verse, such as "Make me to know your ways, O LORD; teach me your paths" (Psalm 25:4).

A Way to Begin

Invite group members to name some things—relationships, talents, or possessions—that are important to them. If they have brought some possessions that are important to them on the camping trip, ask them to show what they brought.

Something to Do

Remind group members of the difficult choices they may have made in packing for this camping trip. There wasn't space to bring every book, toy, or item of clothing they owned! Ask them to go get one important possession from their tent, sleeping area, or cabin. When everyone returns, take turns inviting each person to show the item and explain its importance. When everyone has had the opportunity to "show and tell," ask questions such as the following:

- What makes something important to you?
- What important things couldn't you fit in a duffel bag or bring in a backpack?
- How do we make decisions about what is more important than something else?

Bible Discovery

Introduce the parable of the rich man. Explain that Jesus told this parable to help his listeners think about what was really important. Tell, read, or act out this story. Older children may read Luke 12:13-21 from a contemporary version of the Bible.

A very rich man had an extremely good harvest one year. He harvested so much corn and grain that he did not have room in his barns to store all of it. So he decided to take down the barns he had and build bigger ones. The man was very pleased with how many things he had and the money he could earn so he could buy more things. So he relaxed and decided he didn't need to work but could party for a long time. However, that very night he died. "Now," asked Jesus, "who owns all his possessions, and what good do they do him? He should have stored up good things for God."

After hearing the parable, ask questions such as the following:

- What do you think about the rich man? Was he smart or not? Why?
- What do you think Jesus wants us to understand about what is important?
- What do you think can help us decide what is important here at the campsite and after we go home?

Prayer (Together)

You can use the words of this prayer, or see Creating Family Prayers on page 10.

God our provider, forgive us when we take more than we need. Help us to make good decisions about what is important. Amen.

Parable of the Talents
Matthew 25:14-30
THEME: *Caring for God's good gifts*

Claim the Time

As a signal for the beginning of devotional time, sing a simple song, such as "Seek Ye First," or one verse of "Tell Me the Story of Jesus." Or you can say a Psalm verse, such as "Make me to know your ways, O LORD; teach me your paths" (Psalm 25:4).

A Way to Begin

Encourage group members to look around and to name good gifts from God they can see or hear in creation. Ask one person to write down what everyone says.

Something to Do

Invite group members to think about the list of good gifts and then to name one way they can take care of the things everyone named. For example, if someone said birds, then think of a way everyone can take care of birds. Explain that taking care of God's gifts is called stewardship. Then ask everyone to think of gifts from God that aren't found in nature. Examples might include family fun, toys, pets, computer games, favorite foods, and friends. Write these down, and then think of ways everyone can take care of these gifts. When the list of ways to care for gifts is complete, ask questions such as the following:

- What are some of the ways you can take care of God's gifts in creation?
- Why do you think God want us to take good care of God's gifts?
- Which of God's gifts is it most difficult for you to take care of?

Bible Discovery

Introduce the parable of the talents. Explain that Jesus told this parable to help his listeners think about how they use the resources that God has given to them. Tell, read, or act out this story. Older children can read Matthew 25:14-30 from a contemporary version of the Bible.

Once there was a rich man who planned to go away on a business trip. He called three of his workers together and gave them some of his money to take care of. He gave one man $5,000, another $2,000, and another $1,000. The man who received $5,000 traded with it and earned another $5,000; the man who received $2,000 also doubled the money; but the one who received $1,000 was afraid he would lose the money, so he put it in a hole in the ground. When the rich man returned, he was very happy to learn that the first two men had doubled his money. And he was very unhappy that the third man had put the $1,000 in the ground. The rich man called this worker lazy, gave his money to the one with $10,000, and fired him.

After sharing the parable, ask questions such as the following:

- Why do you think the owner gave $1,000 to the man with the most money?
- If someone gave you a lot of money, what would you do with it?
- What are some of the ways we can care for what God has given us when we go home?

Prayer (Together)

You can use the words of this prayer, or see Creating Family Prayers on page 10.

God of creation, thank you for the wonderful world you gave us to care for. Help me to be a good caretaker of your world. Amen.

Parable of the Good Samaritan

Luke 10:25-37

THEME: *Neighbors*

Claim the Time

As a signal for the beginning of devotional time, sing a simple song, such as "Seek Ye First," or one verse of "Tell Me the Story of Jesus." Or you can say a Psalm verse, such as "Make me to know your ways, O LORD; teach me your paths" (Psalm 25:4).

A Way to Begin

Encourage group members to tell who some of their neighbors are. Ask them to share some of the ways in which they are good neighbors to these people.

Something to Do

Take a walk around your campsite and the surrounding area. Invite everyone to name a neighbor—including not just people but also animals and other living elements of creation. Brainstorm together about ways in which your family group can be a good neighbor to all creatures—humans, animals, and plants at the campsite. Take notes so that you can then challenge each person to choose one specific thing to do today to be a good neighbor at the campsite. After everyone has decided on an action, ask questions such as the following:

- Who has been a good neighbor to you today?
- How does it feel when someone is a good neighbor to you?
- What is the best way to thank someone who has been a good neighbor to you?

Bible Discovery

Introduce the parable of the good Samaritan. Explain that Jesus told this parable to help his listeners think about who is a good neighbor. Tell everyone that in Jesus' day Samaritans were disliked and treated as outsiders. Tell, read, or act out this story. Older children may read Luke 10:25-37 from a contemporary version of the Bible.

A man was going down the road to Jericho. Robbers came and beat him up, took his money, and left him wounded on the roadside. Soon a priest came down the road and saw the hurt man but walked by. Another religious person came down the road and also walked by on the other side of the road. Finally, a third man came down the road. He was a Samaritan—someone the Jews disliked because he was a foreigner and worshiped God in a different way. However, the Samaritan felt sorry for the hurt man, put bandages on his cuts, and took him to a motel. At the motel he fed the hurt man and paid for him to stay there until he was better.

After sharing the parable, ask questions such as the following:

- Why was it such a surprise that the Samaritan became the good neighbor?
- Why do you think the two other men decided not to help the hurt man?
- What stops you from helping others?
- What kind of a neighbor would you like to be when you get home?

Prayer (Together)

You can use the words of this prayer, or see Creating Family Prayers on page 10.

God, thank you for people who are good neighbors to us. Help me to be a good neighbor too, not only to my human neighbors but to all of creation. Amen.

S'mores and More

Kid-friendly Camping Recipes

More S'mores

Some fun twists on the classic recipe found on page 11.

- Spread peanut butter (~1 T.) on each graham cracker before sandwiching the toasted marshmallow and/or chocolate.
- Use chocolate-covered or cinnamon graham crackers for more a flavorful sandwich.
- Make other toppings available to sprinkle on your melted marshmallows—cinnamon, nutmeg, brown sugar, rainbow or chocolate sprinkles, chopped nuts, etc.
- Add your favorite fruit to the S'more—and try to convince yourself that it's healthy now! Bananas, strawberries, blueberries, and even coconut make for fun additions.
- Use other thin chocolates or easily melted candies to enliven the classic S'more:
  - Andes Thins in Crème de Menthe, Cherry Jubilee, Mint Parfait, or Toffee Crunch varieties
  - Tootsie Rolls in original or fruit flavors
  - Caramels, regular or Goetze's caramel creams
  - Ghiardelli Squares in solid chocolate (dark, white, milk) or filled varieties (caramel, mint, raspberry, peanut butter)
  - Reese's Peanut Butter Cups, now in milk, white, and dark chocolate

Trail Mix

Let children create their own trail mix before going on a hike or heading off for a swim. Assume 1/2 to 1 cup of mix per serving. Consider adding some of these creative sweet or savory options to the classic "good old raisins and peanuts" (gorp).

- Craisins, or dates
- Dried pineapple, papaya, bananas, apricots, or apples
- Cashews, walnuts, almonds, or macadamia nuts
- Chocolate, peanut butter, butterscotch, or carob chips
- Sunflower or pumpkin seeds
- Favorite dry cereal (Chex, Cheerios, etc.)

Fun with Camp Dough

Using the recipe for camp dough below, let kids try some of these recipes over your campfire, grill, or stove.

2 cups all-purpose flour
3 tbsp. dried milk powder
1 1/2 tsp. cream of tartar
1/2 tsp. baking soda
1/4 cup margarine or butter
3/4 cup water

Combine dry ingredients and then rub the margarine or butter into them until the mixture looks and feels like coarse meal. (You can keep the "meal" in a sealed plastic bag until needed; it will travel well for as long as 3 days.) Add water and stir just until dough is sticky. Do not add too much water or overmix. Makes 2 1/2 cups.

- Use the dough to make biscuits or pizza dough on your camp stove or over the coals.
- Wrap 1 piece of string cheese in a flat, rectangle of dough (~1/4 inch thick) and seal edges tightly. Wrap the "log" in a buttered section of double-thick aluminum foil and place on grill or coals, turning regularly for 12–18 minutes until dough is cooked through.

- Precook hot dogs for 2–4 minutes by putting them in foil on the coals. Pat small fist-sized balls of dough into thin rectangles. Allow children to wrap the cooled hot dogs in their dough blankets.
  —On grill, brush dough lightly with vegetable oil or melted butter before placing hot dogs on rack.
  —For campfires, wrap each dog in a blanket in buttered foil, double thickness with the shiny side touching the food.
  —Turn regularly to ensure the dough is cooked evenly and completely.

Campfire Mac-n-Cheese

In advance, boil water and cook pasta according to package directions. Elbow macaroni, small shells, or rotini are kid favorites. For each serving, you will need:

  1 small aluminum pie pan (~4¹/2 inch)
  ¹/2 cup pre-cooked pasta
  ¹/4 cup shredded cheddar cheese
  1 tbsp. grated parmesan cheese
  1 tbsp. milk
  ¹/2 tbsp. butter or margarine
  Salt and pepper to taste

Allow children to combine the ingredients in their own pan. Seal the pan tightly with a double-thickness of aluminum foil. If you use a 12 x 16-inch sheet of foil, you can use the extra length to create a sturdy handle over the top, through which you can easily poke a stick or tongs. Cook over flames of fire or grill for about 7 minutes or until cheese has melted. Remove from fire and allow to cool briefly. Open carefully and stir before eating.

Creepy-Crawly Rice and Beans

2 cups uncooked rice (wild rice is best!)
1 can black beans
1 can French-cut green beans
1 cup fresh shredded carrots

Engage children's imaginations while getting them to eat their vegetables with this playful variation on the campfire classic of rice and beans. Boil water over fire and cook rice according to package directions. Add the black beans (bugs), green beans (snakes), and carrots (worms).

Campfire Chili

1 lb. ground beef or turkey (optional)
1 can white or chili beans
1 can red kidney beans
1 can crushed tomatoes
2 cans condensed tomato soup
Chili powder, salt, pepper, garlic to taste
Cheddar or Monterrey Jack cheese, if desired

For meat eaters, brown meat and drain the grease. Vegetarians can start with just the beans, tomatoes, and soup. Stir in seasonings to taste, and add water to stretch the recipe after a particularly strenuous day! Simmer for 1–2 hours. Garnish with crumbled or shredded cheese. This is great with cornbread or biscuits on the side.

Kid-Sized Veggies

Baby corn
Grape tomatoes
Broccoli florets
Miniature carrots
Brussel sprouts ("baby cabbage"), etc.
Garlic, cloves or powder, to taste
Olive oil

Provide a selection of "miniature" vegetables and allow the children to help you toss them together with a little oil and garlic on a large sheet of aluminum foil. Seal the foil tightly and roast for 20–30 minutes over campfire or grill.

Fire Fries

4 to 6 large potatoes or yams
Seasoning of choice (Old Bay, Lawry's)
Non-stick cooking spray
Heavy-duty aluminum foil

A great complement to the traditional campfire barbeque! Cut baking potatoes or yams into French-fry dimensions. Coat them lightly with cooking spray and place in center of the shiny side of a heavily spray-coated sheet of aluminum foil. Season to taste. Seal tightly and roast over camp stove or grill for 45 minutes.